NUTCASES

EQUITY AND TRUSTS

AUSTRALIA
LBC Information Services
Sydney

CANADA and USA
Carswell
Toronto · Ontario

NEW ZEALAND
Brooker's
Auckland

SINGAPORE and MALAYSIA
Thomson Information (S.E. Asia)
Singapore

NUTCASES

EQUITY AND TRUSTS

FIRST EDITION

by

CHRIS CHANG
LL.B, Barrister (U.K.),
Advocate and Solicitor (Malaysia)
Senior Lecturer, LL.B Programme Leader
School of Law, Middlesex University

JOHN WELDON
LL.B, LL.M Dip. A & S Law
Principal Lecturer
School of Law, Middlesex University

London · Hong Kong · Dublin
Sweet & Maxwell
1997

Published in 1997 by
Sweet & Maxwell Limited
of 100 Avenue Road
London, NW3 3PF

Phototypeset by J&L Composition Ltd, Filey, North Yorkshire
Printed in England by Clays Ltd, St Ives plc

No natural forests were destroyed to make this product:
only farmed timber was used and re-planted

ISBN 0 421 597003

**A CIP catalogue record for this book is available
from the British Library**

CONTENTS

TABLE OF CASES

TABLE OF STATUTES

1. INTRODUCTION TO EQUITY AND TRUSTS

What is Equity?

Essentially, equity is the law which prior to the *Supreme Court of Judicature Acts 1873 and 1875* was applied by the Chancellor and subsequently by the Court of Chancery. Maitland has said that equity is a jurisdiction which is supplementary to, or, a gloss on the common law. The nature and development of the law is such that it is not possible to give a definitive explanation of what equity is.

"Equity is no part of the law, but a moral virtue, which qualifies, moderates and reforms the rigour, hardness and edge of the law, and is a universal truth; it does also assist the law where it is defective and weak . . . and defends the law from crafty evasions, delusions, and new subtleties, invented and contrived to evade and delude the common law. . . . Equity therefore does not destroy the law nor create it but assist it." *per* Sir Nathan Wright in *Lord Dudley v. Lady Dudley* (1705) Prec. Ch. 241.

Fusion of Common Law and Equity

The Supreme Court of Judicature Acts 1873 and 1875 fused the administration of common law and equity.

KEY PRINCIPLE: *There is some suggestion that the Supreme Court of Judicature Acts 1873 and 1875 have fused the substantive systems of common law and equity.*

United Scientific Holdings Ltd v. Burnley Borough Council 1977

The issue was whether the time table specified in a rent review clause in a lease for the completion of various steps for the determination of the new rent payable, in the absence of a contrary intention, was of essence to the contract.

HELD: (HL) In the absence of a contrary intention, the time-table specified in a rent review clause for the completion of various steps for the determination of the new rent was not of the essence to the contract. [1978] A.C. 904

COMMENTARY
The decision itself is not important for present purposes. It is the dictum of Lord Diplock with regard to the question of whether there is fusion of the common law and equity which is of interest. Lord Diplock stated (pp. 924–925) that " . . . [t]he innate conservatism of English lawyers may have made them slow to recognise that by the Judicature Act 1873 the two systems of substantive and adjectival law formerly administered by Courts of Law and Courts of Chancery were fused". This dictum has been widely criticised and the better view appears to be that the two systems of common law and equity are not fused but there has been an influence of one system on the other in its development, such that, the two systems of common law and equity may be coming closer together but they are not yet fused. Indeed, many academics such as Hayton have argued that the common law and equity cannot be fused because legal and equitable rights, interests and remedies are different, and therefore it is wrong to say that the two are fused.

Trusts Distinguished from other Concepts

[a] Trusts compared with contracts

KEY PRINCIPLE: *The presence of a contract does not prevent a trust from arising.*

Barclays Bank Ltd v. Quistclose Investments Ltd 1970
(See Chap. 7)

HELD: (HL) Where the money had been given for a specific purpose which could not be carried out, the money was to be held on a resulting trust for the party providing the money. [1970] A.C. 567

COMMENTARY
Notwithstanding the presence of the contract for the loan, a resulting trust arose where the purpose for which the money

was given had failed. This makes it clear that the presence of a contract does not prevent a trust from arising.

[b] Trusts compared with gifts

KEY PRINCIPLE: *Where an intended gift fails, equity will not presume that a trust was intended.*

Jones v. Lock 1865

A father handed a cheque to his nine-month old son stating that "I give this to baby for himself". He then immediately removed the cheque for safekeeping. Although steps were taken to see his solicitor, the father died before he could set up a trust for his son. The cheque was found amongst the father's personal effects.

HELD: (CA in Ch.) Although there was an intention to make an outright gift, the attempt to make such a gift failed and in the absence of an intention to set up a trust, a trust could not be implied. (1865) L.R. 1 Ch. App. 25

COMMENTARY

Equity is reluctant to find the existence of a trust where an intended gift fails. However, there may be situations where an intention to create a trust could be inferred, in which case, the court may be prepared to find the existence of a trust. In the case itself, the court was reluctant to find that loose talk by the father could give rise to a trust.

KEY PRINCIPLE: *There must be a serious intention to create a trust.*

Lambe v. Eames 1871

(See Chap. 4).

HELD: (CA in Ch.) The words used by the testator were insufficient to give rise to a trust. The gift to the widow was an absolute gift. [1871] 6 Ch. App. 597

COMMENTARY

If the court found that a trust existed, the gift to the illegitimate son would have been invalid. However, the court decided the use of precatory words, such as the ones used in the case, imposed merely a moral as opposed to a legal obligation on the donee.

[c] Trusts and powers

KEY PRINCIPLE: *One of the essential differences between a trust and a power is that a trust is mandatory (i.e. it imposes a duty on the trustee) whereas a power is discretionary.*

Burroughs v. Philcox 1840

In his will, a testator left property for his two children for life and gave the survivor the power to dispose of the property amongst the testator's nephews and nieces or their children, either all to one of them, or, to as many as the surviving child should think proper.

HELD: (Ch.) This gave rise to a trust with a power of selection. Upon the failure of the survivor of the two children to exercise the power, the estate was distributed to the nephews and nieces in equal shares. (1840) 5 My. & Cr. 72

COMMENTARY
Lord Cottenham decided that a trust rather than a power was created on the facts of the case. His Lordship went onto say that the intention will be implemented by fastening a trust onto the property.

KEY PRINCIPLE: *It is a question of intention whether a trust or a power is intended by the settlor or testator.*

Re Weekes' Settlement 1897

A testatrix gave her husband a life interest in some property with the power to dispose of all such property by will amongst their children. The will did not contain any gift over in default of appointment by the husband. The husband died without exercising the power.

HELD: (Ch.) The testatrix intended to give her husband a mere power rather than impose a trust. Accordingly, the children were not entitled to the property. [1897] 1 Ch. 289

COMMENTARY
If a trust was to have been found to have been intended, then the children would have been entitled to the interest in the property. However, as there was no trust but a mere power, the property went back to her estate on a resulting trust.

[d] Trusts compared with conditional gifts

KEY PRINCIPLE: *It is a matter of construction whether a conditional gift or trust is intended.*

Re Frame 1939
A testator gave all his money and insurance policies to a donee on condition that she adopted the testator's daughter and also gave his son and two other daughters £5 each. The donee was unable to obtain an adoption order.

HELD: (Ch.) The word "condition" used by the testator was not in its strict legal sense. The bequest to the donee was one on trust which the court could enforce. [1939] 2 All E.R. 865

COMMENTARY
It is clear that the words used to create what is allegedly a conditional gift is not necessarily conclusive. It is a matter of construction as to whether what was intended was a trust or a conditional gift. As Simonds J. stated (at 867) " . . . [a] devise or bequest, on condition that the devisee or legatee makes certain payments does not import a condition in the strict sense of the word, but a trust."

2. EQUITABLE DOCTRINES

Introduction

The equitable doctrines and maxims are interlinked and were evolved in the Court of Chancery. The equitable maxims are not considered as a discreet chapter but is considered in the context where they arise.

[A] SATISFACTION

Satisfaction of Ordinary Debts by Legacies

KEY PRINCIPLE: *Where a testator leaves a legacy to a creditor, the presumption is that the legacy is intended to satisfy the debt.*

Talbot v. Duke of Shrewsbury 1714

The Master of Rolls stated that if one being indebted to another in a sum of money does by his will give him as great or greater sum of money that the debt amounts to, without taking any notice at all of the debt, the legacy will nonetheless be in satisfaction of the debt. (1714) Prec. Ch. 394.

COMMENTARY

No facts were given in this case. The general principle is that in appropriate cases, where a legacy is left to a creditor, provided it is more than the debt, then the legacy can be presumed to be in satisfaction of the debt.

KEY PRINCIPLE: *The presumption that the legacy is intended to satisfy a debt will not apply where the debt is more than the legacy.*

Atkinson v. Webb (1704)

An employer gave her employee a bond to pay her £20 per annum, quarterly for life free from tax. By her will, the employer left the employee £20 per annum payable half yearly but subject to tax.

HELD: The gift in the will was not as beneficial as the bond and therefore could not be regarded as satisfaction of the bond. The employee was entitled to take the gift and claim under the bond. (1704) 2 Vern. 478

COMMENTARY

However, in *Fitzgerald v. National Bank Ltd* [1929] 1 K.B. 394, where the debt was more than the legacy, it was held that satisfaction applied.

KEY PRINCIPLE: *The presumption that the legacy is intended to satisfy a debt will not apply where the debt and the legacy are of a different nature or there is some other difference.*

Eastwood v. Vinke 1731

The testator gave a bond on his marriage to, either, settle lands worth £100 per annum on his wife within four months of the marriage, or that his heirs, executors or administrators should within four months after his death pay to his wife the sum of £2,000. The testator left his wife realty worth £88 per annum in his will.

HELD: The legacy could not be taken as satisfaction of the bond. (1731) 2 P. Wms. 613

COMMENTARY
The Master of the Rolls stated (at 616) that " . . . the court has never yet construed a devise of land to be satisfaction for a debt of money . . . ". Thus, where the legacy and the debt are of a different nature one cannot be taken as satisfaction of the other.

KEY PRINCIPLE: *The presumption that the legacy is intended to satisfy a debt will not apply where the legacy is not as beneficial as the payment of the debt.*

Re Horlock 1895
The testator owed a creditor the sum of £300. The debt was repayable within three months after his death. In his will the testator left the creditor £400. As no mention was made as to when the legacy was to be paid, it was paid within a year.

HELD: (Ch.) The legacy could not be taken as being in satisfaction of the debt. [1895] 1 Ch. 516

COMMENTARY
[1] Where the legacy is not as beneficial as the payment of the debt, satisfaction doesn't apply. In this case there was evidence that the testator intended the legacy to be in addition to the debt. However, a contrary view can be seen in *Re Rattenberry* [1906] 1 Ch. 667.
[2] The doctrine of satisfaction of ordinary debts by legacies does not likewise apply where the debt came into existence after the will was executed: *Adams v. Lavender* (1824) M'cle. Yo. 41.

Satisfaction of Portion by Legacies and Ademption of Legacies by Portions

KEY PRINCIPLE: *The doctrine of satisfaction of a portion debt by a legacy can be explained on the basis that "equity leans against double portions".*

Thynne v. Earl of Glengall 1848

A father covenanted to settle a sum of money under a marriage settlement on the occasion of the marriage of his daughter. He later transferred some stock to the trustees of the settlement. In his will, he left a share of his residue to the trustees of the settlement but on trusts which differed from the marriage settlement.

HELD: (HL) The covenant to settle was satisfied by the legacy in the will even though the trusts differed from those of the marriage settlement. (1848) 2 H.L.C. 131

COMMENTARY

The presumption applies because equity will assume that the testator did not intend to benefit the beneficiary (usually a child of the testator) twice. The assumption is that the testator intended to maintain equality among all his children and not to benefit one at the expense of the other.

KEY PRINCIPLE: *The doctrine of satisfaction of a portion debt by a legacy can be rebutted by evidence to the contrary.*

Re Tussaud's Estate 1878

Under a marriage settlement, the settlor gave his daughter a general power of appointment over the trust property. This power was subject to the consent of the trustees. The settlement contained provisions whereby in default of appointment, the daughter and her husband were given life interests, thereafter to the children for life and the remainder to the husband. When the settlor died, he left the daughter a life interest with the remainder to her children and thereafter to her brothers absolutely.

HELD: (CA) The legacy in the will could not be taken to be in satisfaction of the marriage settlement. This was because the legacy and the settlement were entirely different. [1878] 9 Ch. D. 363

COMMENTARY

The evidence sufficient to rebut the application of the doctrine can arise either impliedly, as in the present case, or expressly. In *Ford v. Tynte* (1864) 2 H. & M. 324, the court decided that the doctrine of satisfaction did not apply because there was clear evidence that the testator intended the child to take both the portion debt and the legacy.

KEY PRINCIPLE: *The doctrine of satisfaction of a portion debt by a legacy does not apply where the nature of the portion debt or its limitation is different from the legacy unless the difference is slight.*

Russell v. St Aubyn 1876

The limitation contained in a settlement differed from the limitation contained in the will. The question arose as to whether the legacy could be taken as satisfaction of the settlement.

HELD: (Ch.) The presumption that the legacy was in satisfaction of the settlement was not rebutted by the difference of the limitations in the settlement and the will, having regard to the subject matter. (1876) 2 Ch. D. 398

COMMENTARY

Where the difference in the nature of the subject matter or the limitation of the portion and the legacy is slight, the doctrine of satisfaction will apply. Where there is a difference in the nature of the subject matter or the limitation, it was said in *Bellasis v. Uthwatt* (1737) 1 Atk. 426, that with respect to the doctrine of satisfaction, the thing given in satisfaction must be of the same nature and certainty as the portion. His Lordship went onto say that land is not to be taken in satisfaction of money and vice versa.

KEY PRINCIPLE: *The doctrine of ademption applies where the legacy or gift in the will is deemed to have been adeemed by a portion gift during the testator's lifetime.*

Re Furness 1901

A testator executed a will in 1885 in which he left his daughter the sum of £20,000 upon the daughter attaining the age of 25 or marriage prior to that age, £15,000 of it was to be settled for her and her children's benefit. When the daughter married in 1893, he settled £7,300 consols for her and her children, although this was different from that declared in the will.

HELD: (Ch.) The £7,300 consols must be taken as partial ademption of the legacy in the will. [1901] 2 Ch. 346

COMMENTARY
This is the reverse of the situation of satisfaction of a portion by a legacy. In the case of ademption, it is the legacy in the will which is adeemed (or partially adeemed) by the portion given by the testator during his lifetime.

KEY PRINCIPLE: *The presumption of satisfaction is easier to rebut than the presumption of ademption.*

Lord Chichester v. Coventry 1867

B covenanted under a marriage settlement to pay to trustees the sum of £10,000 three months after demand with interest payable until payment. This sum was neither demanded nor paid, but interest was paid. B subsequently made a will in which he directed his trustees to pay his debts and legacies and to divide the residue between his daughters. The trusts of the settlement were different from the trusts in the will.

HELD: (HL) The doctrine of satisfaction did not apply here. The gift in the will was not satisfaction of B's covenant in the marriage settlement. Therefore, the £10,000 had to be paid before the residue was divided between the daughters. (1867) 2 L.R. 71 H.L.

[B] CONVERSION

Introduction

Since January 1, 1997, the doctrine of conversion in respect of trusts of land has been abolished: section 3 of the *Trusts of Land and Appointment of Trustees Act 1996* ("*TLATA 1996*"). Where trusts of land are not involved, the doctrine of conversion still applies.

KEY PRINCIPLE: *The application of the equitable maxim "equity deems that as done what ought to be done" means that in some situations an interest in land is deemed to be personalty or vice versa.*

Fletcher v. Ashburner 1779

The testator left his house and his personal estate to trustees on trust to sell so much of it as shall be necessary to pay his debts and then for his wife for life and thereafter to sell the property and divide it between his son and daughter. In the event that either of the children predeceased the testator's wife, the survivor was entitled to the estate absolutely. The daughter and then the son predeceased the testator's wife. The son's heir at law applied for a conveyance of the real property devised by the will. The next of kin claimed to be entitled to the house because the direction to sell the real property converted it into personalty.

HELD: The next of kin were entitled to the property as the direction to sell had converted the real property into personalty. (1779) 1 Bro. C.C. 497

KEY PRINCIPLE: *The doctrine of conversion may apply in cases where an option to purchase land has been given.*

Lawes v. Bennett 1785

The freehold owner of a farm leased it to D for seven years and at the same time gave him an option to purchase the farm at an agreed price expiring on September 29, 1765. The freeholder died in 1763 and by his will left the personalty to the plaintiff and defendant equally and the realty to the defendant. The option to purchase was exercised prior to its expiry in 1765 and the proceeds of sale was paid to the defendant.

HELD: The proceeds from the sale of the farm should go to the plaintiff and defendant equally as the exercise of the option related back to the grant of the option. The doctrine of conversion operated from the date of the grant and therefore would be treated as personalty from that date. (1785) 1 Cox. Eq. Cas. 167

COMMENTARY
[1] This case has been subject to much criticism. Later decisions have tended to interpret the case strictly on its facts.

Thus, where the property is specifically left to a beneficiary instead of being a residuary gift, the principle in *Lawes v. Bennett* does not apply: *Weeding v. Weeding* (1861) 1 John & H. 424 and *Re Pyle* [1895] 1 Ch. 724. However, the principle has been held to apply in the case of a specific bequest of shares and the subsequent exercise of the option to purchase the shares by a third party: *Re Carrington* [1932] 1 Ch. 1.

[2] The doctrine of conversion may also apply in cases where there is an agreement for the sale of land and the remedy of specific performance is available. The operation of the doctrine of conversion in such a case is deemed to convert the interest of the vendor from an interest in land to an interest in personalty. However, this does not apply where specific performance is unavailable: *Thomas v. Howell* (1886) 34 Ch. D. 166.

[C] ELECTION

KEY PRINCIPLE: *The application of the doctrine of election is not dependent on the intention of the testator.*

Re Mengel's Will Trusts 1962

A testator who was domiciled in Denmark at the time of his marriage, left a will in which he, *inter alia*, gave his niece his library of books and to his nephew his collection of etchings and mountain photographs. The question arose as to whether these two gifts were valid in view of the fact that as he was domiciled in Denmark at the relevant time, there was community of property between the testator and his wife.

HELD: (Ch.) The application of the doctrine of election is applied because a mistake was made by the testator who had clearly shown an intention to dispose of property of another. As there was community of property between the testator and his wife, and the testator had given property to his nephew and niece which no longer belonged to him, the doctrine of election applied. [1962] 1 Ch. 791

COMMENTARY

The doctrine of election usually applies where the testator has made a mistake as to his ownership of the property in question. His intention is not generally relevant so long as it is clear that the testator did attempt to dispose of property which he does not own whether intentionally or otherwise.

KEY PRINCIPLE: *The property which the testator wrongfully attempts to dispose of must be available for transfer to the third party.*

Re Lord Chesham 1886

A testator left various chattels upon trusts for sale for the benefit of his two younger sons and the residue of his estate to his eldest son in his will. The chattels were however, heirlooms which were settled by an earlier deed in which the eldest son was the tenant for life. The question arose whether the eldest son was put to election and therefore had to compensate his younger brothers.

HELD: (Ch.) The eldest son was not bound to compensate his younger brothers as he did not have any interest in the chattels. The chattels were not available for transfer to the younger sons. The doctrine of election did not apply. (1886) 31 Ch. D. 466

COMMENTARY
Where the testator has wrongly disposed of property which is not his, the doctrine of election does not apply if that property is not freely available for disposal by the person who is put to his election. The same conclusion was reached in *Re Gordon's Will Trusts* [1978] Ch. 145.

KEY PRINCIPLE: *The doctrine of election will apply even where the person who is put to election can contribute only part of the subject matter of the gift.*

Re Dicey 1957

A testatrix left two freehold houses to her grandson, J, in her will. In the same will she gave her son another freehold house and the residue of her real and personal estate. The testatrix did not have any interest in the two freehold houses which she could dispose of. She occupied them merely as a life tenant under a deed of family arrangement. Under this, her son was entitled to a half share of the beneficial interest in the two freehold houses, with J and his brother, C, being entitled to a quarter share each. J argued that the testatrix's son must elect.

HELD: (CA) The testatrix's son had to elect notwithstanding that J would only be entitled to no more that a three quarter share in the houses and therefore took only part of the testatrix's intended gift. [1957] Ch. 145

COMMENTARY
Even though the intended donee of the gift does not obtain the whole gift under the doctrine of election, the person who is put to election will nonetheless have to elect.

KEY PRINCIPLE: *Where a testator is one of two tenants in common of a property and leaves that property to a third party, whilst leaving a legacy for the other tenant in common, that tenant in common is put to election.*

Padbury v. Clarke 1850
The testator was one of two tenants in common in a property and he left the whole of the property to a third party in his will. In the same will he left a legacy for the other tenant in common.

HELD: (Ch.) Since it was clear that the testator intended to leave the whole of the property to the third party, the other tenant in common was put to election. (1850) 2 Macq. & G. 298

KEY PRINCIPLE: *The doctrine of election is tested at the time of the testator's death.*

Re Edwards 1958
A testatrix, by her will, left a house and the residue of her estate to be divided between seven of her relatives which included her sister. After the execution of the will, the testatrix entered into an agreement with her sister to transfer the house to her for valuable consideration. The house was subsequently conveyed to the sister. The question was whether the sister was put to election.

HELD: (Ch.) The sister was not put to election. The transfer of the house to the sister adeemed the devise in the will. [1958] Ch. 168

COMMENTARY
In the case of a will, the doctrine of election is applied to the state of affairs which exists at the time of the testator's death.

Thus, if any of the conditions giving rise to the doctrine of election is not satisfied at that time, there is no need to elect. See also *Grissell v. Swinhoe* (1869) L.R. 5 Eq. 291.

KEY PRINCIPLE: *Where the testator has a special power of appointment in favour of a limited class but fails to make an appointment in favour of that class, but instead appoints in favour of a stranger, the testator is to be regarded as attempting to dispose of property which should belong to those entitled in default. If those entitled in default of appointment are left property by the testator, the doctrine of election may apply.*

Bristow v. Warde 1794

A father had a power of appointment over some stock in favour of his children. In default of appointment, the stock was to go to the children. The testator appointed part of the stock to his children and the remainder to strangers in his will. The testator did not leave any property of his own to the children.

HELD: (Ch.) The children were not put to election as they were not left any property by the testator as compensation. The children were entitled to the stock left to them in the will as well as those given to strangers. (1794) 2 Ves. 336

Whistler v. Webster 1794

The testator appointed in favour of his grandchildren under a power to appoint in favour of his children. In default of appointment, the fund was to go to the children in equal shares. The children were left legacies in the will.

HELD: (Ch.) The children having been left legacies in the testator's will, the doctrine of election applied and therefore the children were put to election. (1794) 2 Ves. Jr. 367

COMMENTARY

In *Whistler v. Webster*, the children were put to an election. The options open to them were either, to take under the will when they would keep the property given to them by the testator but would have to give up all rights to the fund which was wrongly given to the grandchildren, or to take against the will. In the latter situation, the children would not take the property left to them by the testator in his will but would be entitled to claim the fund which was wrongly appointed to the grandchildren.

[D] PERFORMANCE

KEY PRINCIPLE: *The equitable doctrine of performance is where equity will presume that an act which is done by a covenantor is in performance of his covenant.*

Lechmere v. Lady Lechmere 1735

The settlor covenanted that he would buy freehold land worth £30,000 within a year of his marriage and settle it on trust for himself for life, with a jointure in remainder for the defendant, thereafter a remainder to their sons in tail male, with a remainder to the settlor, his heirs and assigns forever. At the time of the marriage the settlor owned some plots of lands in fee simple. He later acquired some life interests and reversionary interests in land. More than a year after his marriage, he bought some fee simple estates but did not settle these on trust for the defendant. The issue arose as to whether any of the purchases of land could be regarded as being in performance of the covenant.

HELD: The land which was owned at the time the covenant was made would not be covered by it. Likewise, the life interests and the reversionary estates did not fall under the covenant as these were of a different nature from that covenanted. However, the fee simple estates purchased subsequently would be regarded as being in performance of the covenant, even though they were bought more than a year after the marriage. (1735) Cas. T. Talb 80

COMMENTARY
This decision is important because it makes it clear that [i] there can be partial performance of a covenant, [ii] that if the property purchased is different in nature from that covenanted there is no performance and [iii] that any property owned by the covenantor prior to the covenant being made would not normally be covered by it.

KEY PRINCIPLE: *The doctrine of performance is also applicable to cases where A promises to pay a sum of money to B on A's death and later dies intestate. If B receives the same* *amount or a greater sum from A's estate on intestacy, this will be deemed to be in performance or partial performance of the covenant.*

Blandy v. Widmore 1716

The covenantor covenanted to leave his wife £650, if she survived him. He died intestate. The wife's share from the distribution of the covenantor's estate was more than £650.

HELD: The wife's share from the distribution would be taken as performance of the covenant. (1716) 1 P. Wms. 323

Oliver v. Brickland 1732

A promised to pay a sum of money within two years of his marriage. In the event of his death, this sum was to be paid by the executors. A died intestate more than two years after his marriage. The question arose whether his widow's share of his estate on intestacy was to be regarded as being in performance of the covenant.

HELD: The widow's share of A's estate on intestacy could not be regarded as performance of the covenant. (1732) cited 3 Atk. 420

COMMENTARY
Although in *Blandy v. Widmore*, the Master of the Rolls stated that the widow's share of the husband's estate was in satisfaction of the covenant, it is a case on the application of the doctrine of performance.

3. EQUITABLE REMEDIES

Specific Performance

KEY PRINCIPLE: *The Court will be prepared to grant the remedy of specific performance where the plaintiff has performed his or her part of the bargain.*

Hart v. Hart 1881

The plaintiff, Mrs Hart, sought an order for the specific performance of an agreement for a separation deed which formed part of the compromise between the parties in earlier divorce proceedings. As a result of the compromise, the plaintiff did not pursue further litigation in respect of the divorce.

HELD: (Ch.) The court had power to enforce specific performance of an agreement to enter into a separation agreement. This agreement was not too vague to be enforced by the court. (1881) 18 Ch. D. 670

KEY PRINCIPLE: *The lack of mutual availability of the remedy of specific performance in a contract will be one of the factors which the court will take into account.*

Price v. Strange 1978

The plaintiff who continued to occupy his maisonette after his underlease had expired, reached an oral agreement with the defendant. It was agreed that in return for the plaintiff carrying remedial works to the property, the defendant would grant him a new underlease at an increased rent. The defendant subsequently repudiated the agreement and refused to allow the plaintiff to continue with the remedial work. However, the defendant continued to accept rent for the next five months. The plaintiff applied for an order of specific performance.

HELD: (CA) Although the plaintiff had not carried out all the remedial work, specific performance was the appropriate remedy. In any case, the defendant had waived her right to claim lack of mutuality by allowing the plaintiff to do some of the remedial work and accepting the increased rent. [1978] Ch. 337

COMMENTARY

Traditionally, the lack of mutual availability of the remedy of specific performance to the parties in the case, was detrimental to an application for the remedy of specific performance: *Flight v. Boland* (1882) 4 Russ. 298. However, it is now regarded as one of the factors the court will take into account in deciding whether to exercise its discretion together with the circumstances prevailing at the date of the hearing.

KEY PRINCIPLE: *Where there is a contract for the sale of ascertained goods, the court has the power to grant specific performance.*

Behnke v. Bede Shipping Co. 1927

The plaintiff who was a shipowner brought an action against the defendant owners of the steamship "City", *inter alia*, for an order for specific performance of a contract. The defendants argued that it was not a case in which specific performance ought to be decreed.

HELD: (KB) Under section 52 of the *Sale of Goods Act 1893* the court may, if it thinks fit, order specific performance of a contract for the sale of a ship. Accordingly, specific performance of the contract would be ordered. [1927] 1 K.B. 649

COMMENTARY

Section 52 (now of the *Sale of Goods Act 1979*) gives the court a power to order specific performance in any action for breach of contract to deliver specific or ascertained goods. However, specific performance of a contract for ascertained or specific goods will be granted only in cases where they are unique, because otherwise, damages will be an adequate remedy. In *Cohen v. Roche* [1927] 1 K.B. 169, the court refused to order specific performance of a contract for the sale of eight Hepplewhite chairs. See also *Falcke v. Gray* (1859) 4 Drew. 651.

KEY PRINCIPLE: *In contracts for the sale of unascertained goods, the court may enforce the contract where the circumstances justify it.*

Sky Petroleum Ltd v. VIP Petroleum Ltd 1974

The plaintiff had an agreement with the defendant for the supply of all their requirements of petrol and diesel at a fixed price. At a time when supplies were restricted, and where it was unlikely that the plaintiff could find an alternative supplier, the defendant terminated the contract. The plaintiff sought an injunction to restrain the defendant from withholding supplies.

HELD: (Ch.) That to grant an injunction would in effect be to grant an order for the specific performance of the contract to sell unascertained goods. Such an order would not normally be granted as damages would be an adequate remedy. However, in the circumstances of the case, it was clear that damages would not be an adequate remedy. Accordingly, the injunction would be granted. [1974] 1 W.L.R. 576

COMMENTARY
The court acknowledged that this amounted to granting specific performance of a contract for the sale of unascertained goods. However, the court was of the view that it had jurisdiction to grant specific performance in cases where the circumstances justified it. In *Howard E Perry & Co. Ltd v. British Railways Board* [1980] 1 W.L.R. 1375, the court granted an order for the delivery of 500 tons of steel, as the steel was not readily available on the open market at the time, and damages would not adequately compensate the plaintiff. A different view was taken in *Société Des Industries Metallurgiques SA v. The Bronx Engineering Co. Ltd* [1975] 1 Lloyds Rep. 465, where an injunction was refused to prevent the removal of a piece of machinery which was readily available in the open market.

KEY PRINCIPLE: *The court is reluctant to grant specific performance of a contract to pay money but may do so in appropriate cases.*

Beswick v. Beswick 1968
An uncle agreed to transfer his business to his nephew in consideration of the nephew employing the uncle as a consultant for the rest of his life and to pay his aunt an annuity for life. The agreement, which was between the uncle and nephew, was made in writing. After the uncle's death, the nephew made one payment to the aunt but refused to make other payments. The aunt commenced an action against the nephew in the capacity as the administratrix of her husband's estate and in her own capacity.

HELD: (HL) The aunt, in her capacity as administratrix of her husband's estate was entitled to an order for specific performance of the contract entered into between her husband and the nephew. She could not succeed in her own capacity as she was not a party to the contract and section 56 of the *Law of Property Act 1925* did not change the law to allow her to do so. [1968] A.C. 58

COMMENTARY

The court granted the remedy of specific performance because damages would have been an inadequate remedy. If damages were awarded, the estate would only be granted nominal damages as it had suffered no loss.

KEY PRINCIPLE: *The court is reluctant to grant an order for the specific performance of a contract that require constant supervision.*

Co-operative Insurance Society Ltd v. Argyll Stores (Holdings) Ltd 1997

The defendant had a 35-year lease of a premises and carried on the business of a supermarket. One of the covenants in the lease provided that the defendant would keep the supermarket open for the duration of the lease. The defendant sold the supermarket and stripped out the premises, despite a written notice by the plaintiff to keep it open as a supermarket. The Court of Appeal took the view that damages were an inadequate remedy and granted an order for specific performance. The defendants appealed to the House of Lords.

HELD: (HL) The appeal would be allowed because the practice of not granting orders which compelled a business to continue was based on sound sense and should not be departed. One of the reasons for this was that the court was reluctant to grant an order for specific performance of a contract which required constant supervision. Further the obligation contained in the clause could not be regarded as sufficiently precise to be capable of specific performance. *The Times* May 26, 1997

COMMENTARY

Although the court refused to grant an order for specific performance of the contract in question, in appropriate cases, the court may be willing to do so regardless of the fact that the contract is one which requires constant supervision. The court may be prepared to grant such an order in cases where the contract is clear as to what has to be done. In *Posner v. Scott-Lewis* [1987] Ch. 25, the court ordered a landlord to appoint a resident porter in accordance with the covenants entered into by the landlord, as what had to be done was sufficiently defined.

KEY PRINCIPLE: *In cases of contracts of employment, the court may grant an order of specific performance or equivalent remedy against an employer to continue the employment of the employee, where the employer retains full confidence in the employee's ability.*

Powell v. London Borough of Brent 1987

The plaintiff was promoted to the post of Principal Benefits Officer after an interview. A few days after she reported for work, the defendant informed her that it was not possible to appoint her as there was a possible breach of the equal opportunity code of practice. The plaintiff sought an injunction to restrain the defendant from advertising the post and requiring them to treat her as if she was properly appointed.

HELD: (CA) The plaintiff was entitled to an injunction until the trial of the action. Although as a general rule there can be no specific performance of a contract of service, the present case was an exception to it. The evidence showed that the defendant had full confidence in her ability to do the job. [1987] I.R.L.R. 446

COMMENTARY

[1] *De Francesco v. Barnum* (1890) 45 Ch. D. 430 represents the equitable approach to such contracts where the court was reluctant to grant specific performance of contracts of employment as to do so might be to convert such contracts into contracts of slavery. In cases where an order is sought against the employer, as a general rule, the courts are reluctant to do so.

[2] However, where the employer retains full confidence in the ability of the employee, and where it is just to do so, an order compelling the continued employment of the employee may be granted. See *Hill v. C. A. Parsons & Co. Ltd* [1972] Ch. 305.

KEY PRINCIPLE: *In building contracts, where the work to be carried out is clear, the court may grant a specific performance order.*

Mayor, Aldermen and Burgesses of Wolverhampton v. Emmons 1901

The plaintiffs sold a plot of land abutting a street to the defendant. The defendant covenanted to erect buildings on it within a specified time. Subsequently, it was agreed that the defendant was to erect eight houses in accordance with specified plans. The defendant failed to perform the agreement.

HELD: (CA) The facts of the case fell within the exception to the general rule that specific performance of a building contract will not be ordered. An order would be made for the specific performance of the contract to build the eight houses in accordance with the specified plans. [1901] K.B. 514

COMMENTARY
Romer J. suggested that a building contract would be specifically enforced where three conditions are satisfied. They are:

- the work is sufficiently defined;
- the plaintiff has a substantial interest in the contract being performed such that damages would be an inadequate compensation;
- the defendant is in occupation of the plaintiff"s land in accordance with the contract.

Building contracts not satisfying these criteria may not be specifically enforced because of the need for constant supervision.

KEY PRINCIPLE: *In deciding whether to grant specific performance, the court will take into account the application of the equitable maxims.*

Quadrant Visual Communications Ltd v. Hutchison Telephone (U.K.) Ltd 1993
The defendant agreed to purchase the plaintiff's portable and car telephone business. The consideration was partly calculated on the number of subscribers signing up after the sale. The plaintiff failed to disclose that it had entered into an agreement with a third party for the provision of free portable phones in return for vouchers. The plaintiff sought an order for specific performance of the defendant's contractual obligations.

HELD: (CA) After taking into account the plaintiff's conduct, the court would refuse to grant an order for the specific performance of the defendant's contractual obligations. The plaintiff did not come with clean hands as they failed to disclose the existence of the other agreement. The court's discretion in granting an order for specific performance could not be fettered by a term in the agreement. [1993] B.C.L.C. 442

Patel v. Ali 1984

The defendant husband and wife contracted to sell their house to the plaintiffs. The husband became bankrupt thereby delaying the sale. In the meantime, the wife became ill and whilst pregnant with her second child, had one leg amputated. The husband ended up in prison and the wife later gave birth to a third child. As a result of this, she was dependent on relatives and friends living nearby.

HELD: (Ch.) In the circumstances of the case, the court was justified in refusing specific performance of the contract on the grounds of hardship arising after the contract. Accordingly, it would be just to discharge the order for specific performance. [1984] Ch. 283

COMMENTARY

In deciding whether to grant specific performance, the court has a discretion. It will have regard to the equitable maxims and therefore where the plaintiff's conduct is reprehensible, or where there is hardship, the court can refuse to grant such an order. In *Patel v. Ali*, the court was also prepared to take into account circumstances arising after the contract had been entered into. Other factors which the court takes into account include the doctrine of laches (see *Mills v. Haywood* (1877) 6 Ch. D. 196 and *Lazard Brothers & Co Ltd v. Fairfield Properties Co (Mayfair) Ltd* [1977] 121 S.J. 793), and questions of public policy.

KEY PRINCIPLE: *The court can grant damages in equity in lieu of specific performance.This may be useful where for some reason common law damages are not available.*

Wroth v. Tyler 1974

The plaintiff was the purchaser of a house from the defendant. The purchase could not be completed because the defendant's wife registered a right of occupation under the *Matrimonial Homes Act 1967*. The house was worth £7,500 at the time but its value rose to £11,500 by the time of the trial.

HELD: (Ch.) It was inappropriate to grant specific performance on the facts of the case. However, it was appropriate to award damages in lieu thereof in accordance with Lord Cairns's Act. Damages awarded in equity must be a true substitute for specific performance. Therefore, the damages in this case should be based on the difference in value between the date of the contract and the date of trial. [1973] 1 Ch. 30

Johnson v. Agnew 1978

The defendant contracted to buy a piece of land from the plaintiffs but failed to complete the purchase. The plaintiffs obtained an order for specific performance. Before the order was enforced, the mortgagees of the property took possession and sold the property for a lower price. The plaintiffs then claimed, *inter alia*, for an order that the defendant should pay the balance of the purchase price less the amount from the sale or alternatively, a declaration that the contract had been repudiated and damages at common law. The Court of Appeal ordered that the specific performance order should be set aside and damages awarded in lieu. The defendant appealed.

HELD: (HL) As the order for specific performance could not be complied with, the plaintiff was entitled to apply to the court to end the contract and obtain damages appropriate to the breach of contract. The court could use its power under Lord Cairns's Act to award damages in lieu of specific performance. [1978] Ch. 176

COMMENTARY

The House of Lords in *Johnson v. Agnew* stated that although Lord Cairns's Act allowed for damages to be awarded in some cases where damages were not recoverable at common law, the assessment of damages should nonetheless be on the same basis. The Act did not warrant the assessment of damages otherwise than on a common law basis. Therefore, if *Wroth v. Tyler* is taken as authority that the quantum of damages at common law and equity can be different, that is to be doubted. There is also some doubt whether the damages awarded in *Wroth v. Tyler* could not have been awarded at common law. In the case of a breach of contract, the damages should normally be awarded at the date of the breach of contract. On the facts of *Johnson v. Agnew*, this was the date when specific performance was no longer possible. Where the facts of the case warrants it, a departure from the normal rule is permitted, if it would otherwise cause injustice.

Injunctions

[a] Interlocutory prohibitory injunction

The High Court's jurisdiction to grant interlocutory injunctions comes from section 37 of the *Supreme Court Act 1981* and the County Court's jurisdiction is from section 38 of the *County Courts Act 1984*.

KEY PRINCIPLE: *In deciding whether to grant an interlocutory injunction, the court should take into account various factors.*

American Cyanamid Co. v. Ethicon Ltd 1978

The plaintiffs patented a synthetic absorbable surgical suture. The defendants produced its own synthetic absorbable sutures with a different chemical composition. The plaintiffs applied for an interlocutory injunction to restrain the defendant from selling the sutures.

HELD: (HL) The court should consider the balance of convenience in deciding whether to grant an interlocutory injunction. If there was any doubt as to whether damages would compensate the parties, it was prudent to preserve the status quo. In the circumstances of the case, the injunction should be granted. [1975] A.C. 396

COMMENTARY

The House of Lords suggested that in deciding whether to grant an interlocutory injunction, the court should take into account the following matters:

- whether there is a serious question to be tried;
- the adequacy of damages to the plaintiff and the defendant;
- the balance of convenience—this would include the maintenance of the status quo and any special factors;
- the relative strength of the parties' case, where all the other factors are evenly balanced.

KEY PRINCIPLE: *In applying the American Cyanamid guidelines, the court should avoid having to resolve difficult issues of fact and law. Any view as to the relative strength of the parties' case should be reached only where it is apparent from the affidavit evidence.*

Series 5 Software Ltd v. Clarke 1996

The plaintiffs were the owners of a software package called QC 2000. The defendants, who were the plaintiff's employees removed the software, client lists, the accounts and equipment. They resigned from the company claiming that their salaries had not been paid. The plaintiff applied for an interlocutory order to restrain the defendants from disclosing their trade secrets to third parties or from contacting any of its clients.

HELD: (Ch.) The court should avoid having to resolve difficult issues of fact and law when deciding whether to grant an interlocutory order. Any view as to the relative strength of the parties' case should be reached only where it is apparent from the affidavit evidence. On the facts of the case, having regard to the adequacy or inadequacy of damages and the balance of convenience, it was inappropriate to grant the order. [1996] 1 All E.R. 853

COMMENTARY

Laddie J. stated (at 865) that " . . . [i]n my view Lord Diplock did not intend . . . to exclude consideration of the strength of the parties case in most applications for interlocutory relief. It appears to me that what is intended is that the court should not attempt to resolve difficult issues of fact or law on an application for interlocutory relief. If, on the other hand, the court is able to come to a view as to the strength of the parties' case on the credible evidence, then it can do so". The consideration of the relative strength of the parties' case is not therefore as a last resort. If it is difficult to reconcile this with *American Cyanamid Co. v. Erluicon.*

KEY PRINCIPLE: *The American Cyanamid guidelines are applied with a degree of flexibility.*

Office Overload v. Gunn 1977

The plaintiff applied for an interlocutory injunction against the defendant, who was his employee. The injunction was to restrain the defendant from competing with the plaintiff in accordance with the restraint of trade covenant in the contract of employment for one year.

HELD: (CA) The merits of the case had to be considered as the interlocutory injunction would effectively dispose of the matter since the trial was unlikely to take place until several years after. [1977] F.S.R. 3

COMMENTARY
There are a number of situations where the *American Cyanamid* guidelines are inapplicable. They include:

- where the defendant has no arguable defence (*Patel v. W H Smith (Eziot) Ltd* [1987] 1 W.L.R. 853);
- where there is a likelihood of a defence under section 221 of the *Trade Union and Labour Relations (Consolidation) Act 1992*;
- cases involving public rights (*Secretary of State for the Home Department v. Central Broadcasting Ltd*, The *Times* January 28, 1993);
- where it would finally dispose of the matter (*Cayne v. Global Natural Resources plc* [1984] 1 All E.R. 225);
- applications for interlocutory mandatory injunctions (*Shephard Homes Ltd v. Sandham* [1971] 1 Ch. 340.

KEY PRINCIPLE: *The court can award damages in lieu of an injunction.*

Jaggard v. Sawyer 1995

The defendant, in breach of covenant, built a house. This also resulted in trespass as access to the house was by way of a private road. The plaintiff commenced proceedings for an injunction to restrain use of this private road.

HELD: (CA) In upholding the judge's decision at first instance, the injunction would not be granted as this would cause the house to be landlocked. The injury to the plaintiff was small and it was possible to estimate its value in monetary terms. Further, having regard to the plaintiff's failure to apply for an injunction early on, and the defendant's conduct, it would be oppressive to grant such an injunction. In assessing damages, the court would value the plaintiff's rights at a price which is reasonable for the release or relaxation of the convenant and the grant of a right of way. [1995] 1 W.L.R. 269

COMMENTARY
[1] In this case, damages were awarded in equity which would otherwise not be available at common law. There is no inconsistency with *Johnson v. Agnew*, which, although is authority for the proposition that the assessment of damages

at common law and equity should be the same, their Lordships recognised that one of the exceptions to this was where damages were not available at common law. In the latter situation the court did not have to follow the common law rules. [2] A useful guide as to the award of damages in lieu of injunction is found in the dicta of Smith L.J. in *Shelfer v. City of London Lighting Co.* [1895] 1 Ch. 287. It was suggested that damages would be awarded where:

[a] the injury to the plaintiff was small;
[b] the injury can be valued in monetary terms;
[c] the injury could be compensated adequately by a small payment;
[d] it would be oppressive to grant the injunction.

It must be emphasised that these are merely guidelines and they have not always been universally applied. However, they were applied by the Court of Appeal in *Jaggard v. Sawyer*, above.

[b] Mareva injunctions

KEY PRINCIPLE: *Where there is a likelihood that the defendant may dispose of or remove his assets from the jurisdiction, the court has the jurisdiction to grant an injunction to restrain him from doing so.*

Mareva Compania Naviera SA v. International Bulkcarriers SA 1975

The defendants chartered the plaintiff's ship, the Mareva, which it sub-chartered it to a third party. After having paid two instalments, the defendant defaulted in its payment to the plaintiffs. The plaintiffs obtained an injunction preventing the defendant from disposing or removing any of the moneys which it had received from the third party out of jurisdiction.

HELD: (CA) Where it appeared that a debt was due and owning and there was a danger that the defendant may dispose of its assets so as to defeat the plaintiff's claim, the court had jurisdiction to grant an interlocutory injunction to prevent this. This was a proper case for such an injunction to be granted. [1975] 2 Lloyd's Rep. 509

COMMENTARY
It was said by Lord Diplock in *The Siskina* [1979] A.C. 210, that the purpose of a Mareva injunction was to ensure that a

fund was available within the jurisdiction if the court found in the plaintiff's favour.

KEY PRINCIPLE: *The application for a Mareva injunction should be ancillary to an existing cause of action*

Mercedes Benz AG v. Leiduck 1995

The plaintiff advanced a large sum of money to the defendant for use in a business in Russia. The defendant misappropriated the money. The defendant was detained by a Monaco court and ordered that the defendant's assets in Monaco be frozen. The plaintiff made an *ex parte* application in Hong Kong for a world wide Mareva injunction. The issue arose as to whether the Hong Kong court had jurisdiction to grant such an injunction against a defendant who was out of jurisdiction in support of an action in a foreign jurisdiction.

HELD: (PC) A Mareva injunction could not stand independently of a substantive claim for relief within the court's jurisdiction. [1996] 1 A.C. 284

COMMENTARY

The rule used to be that the court had no jurisdiction to grant a Mareva injunction where it is not ancillary to a cause of action within the jurisdiction of the court. The exception was under section 25 of the *Civil Jurisdictions and Judgments Act 1982* where a High Court has jurisdiction to grant a Mareva injunction in England before the trial or after judgment even though there is no cause of action in England, so long as a court in one of the contracting states has jurisdiction. An example of the application of this provsion is the case of *Credit Suisse Fides Trust Sa v. Cuoghi, The Times*, July 3, 1997. The Court of Appeal refused to discharge a world wide Mareva injunction against a defendant to proceedings in Switzerland, but, who was resident and domiciled in the U.K. Since Switzerland was a Lugano Convention contracting state, and the subject matter of the proceedings was within the Brussels Convention, the court had jurisdiction under section 25 to grant relief. The court noted that nothing in the section prevented it from granting a world wide Mareva injunction. Section 25 has been extended by the *Civil Jurisdiction and Judgments Act 1982 (Interim Relief) Order 1997*, which came into force on April 1, 1997, to cover proceedings commenced or about to be commenced in a non contracting state. Thus if the situation in *Mercedes Benz AG v. Leiduck* were to arise in the U.K., the court can now grant interim relief.

KEY PRINCIPLE: *Specific criteria will have to be satisfied before a Mareva injunction is granted.*

Third Chandris Shipping Corporation v. Unimarine SA 1979

The plaintiffs, who were the respective owners of three ships, had substantial claims against the defendant who had chartered their vessels. They obtained three separate Mareva injunctions restraining the defendant from removing assets, including moneys in its bank account in London.

HELD: (CA) As there were assets within the jurisdiction and there was a real risk that the defendant would dissipate or dispose of its assets before trial, the defendant's application to discharge the injunctions would be dismissed. [1979] 1 Q.B. 645

COMMENTARY
Lord Denning (at 668–669) suggested that certain guidelines must be complied with. The plaintiff should:

- make full and frank disclosure of all material facts which he has knowledge of;
- give particulars of his claim against the defendant;
- give reasons for believing that the defendant has assets within the jurisdiction;
- give grounds for believing that there is a real risk of the assets being disposed of or dissipated before the judgment is satisfied;
- give an undertaking in damages.

KEY PRINCIPLE: *The court has jurisdiction to grant a Mareva injunction covering world wide assets.*

Republic of Haiti v. Duvalier 1990

The plaintiffs commenced action in France against the defendant to recover US$120m alleged to have been embezzled by the defendants. The plaintiffs issued a writ in England, claiming orders restraining the defendants from disposing certain assets and requiring disclosure of their other assets.

HELD: (CA) The court had jurisdiction to grant a Mareva injunction covering world wide assets pending trial of the action. However, cases in which such orders will be granted would be rare. [1990] 1 Q.B. 202

KEY PRINCIPLE: *In granting a Mareva injunction covering world wide assets, the court imposes strict safeguards.*

Derby & Co. Ltd v. Weldon 1989

The plaintiffs commenced an action against the defendants, *inter alia*, for breach of contract, negligence, breach of fiduciary duty, deceit and conspiracy to defraud by, having dealt in cocoa and cocoa futures on their own behalf. The plaintiffs applied for a Mareva injunction covering the first two defendants' assets both within and outside the jurisdiction. The plaintiffs appealed against the decision not to grant the Mareva injunction covering assets outside the jurisdiction.

HELD: (CA) In addition to satisfying the normal criteria for the grant of a Mareva injunction, it was also necessary for the plaintiff to show that any English assets available were insufficient, that there are foreign assets and that there was a real risk of disposal or dissipation of these assets. The court must also be satisfied by undertaking or proviso that the defendant would not be oppressed by exposure to multiplicity of proceedings, be protected against misuse of the information obtained from the disclosure order and that third parties would be adequately protected. In the circumstances of the case, it must be just and convenient to grant a Mareva injunction in relation to the assets of the defendant wherever situated. Accordingly, the Mareva injunction covering the defendants' assets outside the jurisdiction would be granted. [1989] 2 W.L.R. 279

Re BCCI SA (No. 9) 1994

The liquidators of BCCI obtained a Mareva injunction covering world wide assets against an employee and a director of the bank. The issue was whether the order provided adequate safeguards against the multiplicity of proceedings. It was argued that the order should include an undertaking not to commence proceedings in other jurisdictions arising out of the same subject matter.

HELD: (CA) Where a world wide injunction is granted, the plaintiff must undertake not to institute vexatious proceedings against the defendants in arbitrary proceedings world wide. However, liquidators were in a special position and it was normally unnecessary to obtain such an undertaking. Here, it would appear oppressive to allow the liquidators the freedom to initiate proceedings in foreign jurisdictions based on the same subject matter. Therefore, it was reasonable to require the liquidators to give such an undertaking. [1994] 3 All E.R. 764

Derby & Co Ltd v. Weldon (Nos. 3 and 4) 1990
(See above).
The plaintiffs sought a world wide Mareva injunction against the third and fourth defendants. Neither of them appeared to have assets within the jurisdiction.

HELD: (CA) In suitable cases, the court has jurisdiction to grant a Mareva injunction covering foreign assets. The existence of assets within the jurisdiction was not a precondition for the grant of such an injunction. It was an adequate sanction against the defendant that failure to comply with the injunction would result in him being barred from defending the action. Further, as the injunction operated in personam, it did not offend the principle that courts should not make orders infringing the exclusive jurisdiction of other countries. Accordingly, there was jurisdiction to grant a Mareva injunction against the third and fourth defendants. [1990] 1 Ch. 65

COMMENTARY
It is clear that the courts would require that these safeguards are complied with before the court will be prepared to grant a Mareva injunction covering worldwide assets.

KEY PRINCIPLE: *Although a Mareva injunction is an equitable remedy, it operates in rem and can therefore bind third parties.*

Z Ltd v. A-Z and AA-LL 1982
The plaintiffs had been defrauded of large sums of money which was believed to have been paid into accounts at various banks in London. Prior to the issue of the writ, the judge granted Mareva injunctions against 36 defendants, which included six clearing banks. A question arose as to the position of third parties who were served with a Mareva injunction.

HELD: (CA) A Mareva injunction acted *in rem* and therefore everyone with knowledge of the injunction had to comply with the order and was guilty of contempt of court if he assisted in the disposal of the subject matter of the injunction. [1982] 1 Q.B. 558

COMMENTARY
Unlike normal equitable remedies, a Mareva injunction acts both *in rem* and *in personam* (see *Derby & Co. Ltd v. Weldon*, above) and can bind third parties who had been served with notice of the injunction. However, as a safeguard, a plaintiff may be required to undertake to indemnify any third party affected by the order against all reasonably incurred expenses in complying with the order, and all liabilities flowing from this compliance.

[c] Anton Piller orders

KEY PRINCIPLE: *The court has jurisdiction to grant an order allowing for the plaintiff to enter upon the defendant's premises to inspect and remove documents relevant to the case.*

Anton Piller KG v. Manufacturing Processes Ltd 1976

The plaintiff alleged that the defendant, who was its agent in England, had been passing confidential information to a rival company. The plaintiff applied for an interim injunction to restrain the defendants from infringing their copyrights and disclosing confidential information and for an order to enter upon the defendant's premises to inspect and remove relevant documentation.

HELD: (CA) Where the plaintiff had a strong prima facie case of actual or potential serious damage, and there was clear evidence that the defendants possessed documents which they might destroy or dispose of, the court had an inherent jurisdiction to grant an order for the entry, inspection and removal of relevant material from the defendants' premises. [1976] 1 Ch. 55

COMMENTARY
Ormrod L.J. identified three criteria which have to be satisfied before the court can exercise its discretion to grant an Anton Piller order on an *ex parte* application. They are that:

- there must be a strong prima facie case;
- there is serious potential or actual harm to the interests of the plaintiff as a result of the defendant's actions;
- there is clear evidence that the defendant has in his possession incriminating evidence or things and there is a real possibility that this may be destroyed before any inter partes hearing application can be made.

KEY PRINCIPLE: *In cases not involving infringement of intellectual property rights or passing off, the defendant can claim the privilege against self incrimination and refuse to provide the information or documents.*

Tate Access Floors v. Boswell 1991

The plaintiffs alleged that the defendants had defrauded them of large sums of money. They obtained, *inter alia*, an Anton Piller order requiring the defendants to deliver documents within the jurisdiction and to disclose their assets. The defendants applied to set aside the Anton Piller order relying on the privilege against self incrimination.

HELD: (Ch.) The Anton Piller order would be set aside against the first three defendants. Where the privilege against self incrimination applies, it protects the defendant from having to produce and verify documents or information, and would not have to allow the plaintiff entry onto his premises to search for and seize relevant documents. [1991] Ch. 512

COMMENTARY
[1] This problem can be avoided if the plaintiff is able to remove the risk that the information obtained will be used in subsequent criminal proceedings. This is done by securing the written agreement of the Crown Prosecution Service (CPS) that they do not wish to make use of this information. As suggested in *AT&T Istel Ltd v. Tully* [1993] A.C. 45, a suitable clause to this effect must be included in the order. However, such a clause can only be included if the CPS has given its prior written consent: *United Norwest Co-operative Ltd v. Johnstone, The Times*, February 24, 1994.
[2] Where the Anton Piller order may reveal evidence likely to expose the defendant to criminal proceedings, the order must contain a proviso which adequately protects the defendant's right to claim the privilege against self incrimination: *IBM*

United Kingdom Ltd v. Prime Data International Ltd [1994] 4
All E.R. 248.

KEY PRINCIPLE: *In cases involving passing off and/or infringement of intellectual property rights, section 72 of the
Supreme Court Act 1981 prevents the defendant from relying
on the privilege against self incrimination.*

Coca Cola Co. v. Gilbey 1995

P, one of the defendants, applied to discharge an Anton Piller
allowing his premises to be searched in connection with an
alleged infringement of the plaintiff's intellectual property
rights. P alleged that if he provided the information requested
under the order, he would be incriminating himself and expos-
ing himself to the risk of violence.

HELD: (Ch.) P's application would be dismissed as P could
not rely on the privilege against self incrimination in cases
involving infringement of intellectual property rights. Likewise,
the risk of violence to P was not a ground upon which such an
order could be discharged. [1995] 4 All E.R. 711

COMMENTARY
Section 72 of the *Supreme Court Act 1981* removes the privilege of self incrimination where there is an action based on
passing off or infringement of intellectual property rights.

KEY PRINCIPLE: *The courts have imposed strict guidelines
for the execution or enforcement of the Anton Piller order.*

Columbia Picture Industries Inc. v. Robinson 1987

The plaintiffs obtained an Anton Piller against the defendant.
It was alleged that the defendant had infringed the plaintiff's
copyright in films. In the execution of the order, documents and
material were taken, some of which did not form part of the
order. Some items were lost whilst in the plaintiff solicitors'
custody. The defendant applied to set aside the Anton Piller
order and for damages.

HELD: (Ch.) The purpose of the order was to preserve evidence where there was a risk of destruction or disposal of such evidence prior to the trial. The plaintiffs and their solicitors had acted oppressively and abused their powers in the execution of the order by seizing and retaining material not covered by the order and subsequently losing it. It was also inappropriate for the solicitors to retain material where there is a dispute as to its ownership. The originals should be returned, once copies had been made, and a detailed record of material taken must be made prior to its removal from the premises. Consequently, the plaintiffs were liable to the defendants in damages which would be assessed to include aggravated damages. [1987] Ch. 38

COMMENTARY

In *Universal Thermosensors Ltd v. Hibben* [1992] 1 W.L.R. 840, it was suggested that the plaintiffs should be asked to give the following undertakings before the grant of an Anton Piller:

- that the order is served by an independent solicitor who is experienced in the execution of such orders;
- that a written report is prepared by the solicitor executing the order which should be served on the defendant and presented to the court;
- that the order would be served during office hours to give the defendant an opportunity to obtain legal advice;
- that where it is likely that a woman will be at the premises alone, the party serving the order should include a woman.

The Lord Chief Justice subsequently issued the *Practice Direction (ex p. Mareva Injunctions and Anton Piller Orders)* [1994] 4 All E.R. 52 which reinforced the suggestions in *Universal Thermosensors Ltd v. Hibben*, above.

4. CREATION OF EXPRESS PRIVATE TRUSTS

Introduction

To establish a private express trust there must be certainty of intention, subject matter and object. The necessary formalities must be complied with. The trust must be fully constituted in that the property must be properly vested in the trustees in consequence of a declaration of trust.

[A] CERTAINTIES

(i) Certainty of intention

KEY PRINCIPLE: *There must be certainty of intention to create a binding trust. Precatory words will not evince a certain intention.*

Lambe v. Eames 1871

A testator left his estate to his widow. The bequest was phrased "to be at her disposal in any way she may think best, for the benefit of herself and her family". The widow by her will gave part of the estate to an illegitimate son of one of the testator's sons.

HELD: (CA in Ch.) The gift was valid. (1871) 6 Ch. App. 597

Re Adams and the Kensington Vestry 1884

A testator left all his estate to his widow absolutely. The bequest was phrased to be "in full confidence that she would do what was right as to the disposal thereof between the children either in her lifetime or by will after her decease".

HELD: (CA) The wife took an absolute interest in the property unfettered by any trust in favour of the children. (1884) 27 Ch.D. 394

COMMENTARY
In *Lambe v. Eames* the breadth of the wife's discretion was such as to indicate a gift rather than a holding on trust. On the terms of the will the wife could retain or dispose of the property as she thought best. Similarly, in *Re Adams and the Kensington Vestry*, there was no obligation on the wife and hence no claim by any other party to an interest in the property.

KEY PRINCIPLE: *Precatory words may set up a future executory gift.*

Comiskey v. Bowring-Hanbury 1905

A testator left his estate to his widow absolutely. The bequest was phrased to be in full confidence that she would make such use of it as the testator should have made of it and upon her death she would devise it amongst such of her nieces as she thought fit. In default of any disposition by her, during her life or by will, the property was to be equally divided amongst the nieces.

HELD: (HL) There was an absolute gift to the widow subject to an executory gift to such, if any, of the nieces she should choose. [1905] A.C. 84

COMMENTARY

The words used are similar to those in *Re Adams and the Kensington Vestry*, above, where there was held to be no trust. Here, there is a difference. There is no trust binding on the widow during her life because she could dispose of the entire property. There is, however, a potential gift to the nieces whereby they could expect an equal share if the widow made no disposition or, if she did make a disposition, they could expect to be in the class of discretionary beneficiaries.

KEY PRINCIPLE: *Circumstances including a pattern of behaviour or dealing may constitute sufficient evidence of intent to declare a trust.*

Paul v. Constance 1977

The deceased separated from his wife in 1965. In 1967 he set up home with the plaintiff until his death in 1974. In 1969, the deceased received £950 compensation for an industrial injury. This was placed into a deposit account in the deceased's name but money was withdrawn and used for their joint purposes. On several occasions the deceased said: "The money is as much yours as mine." The deceased died intestate and the defendant, who was the widow, claimed his estate.

HELD: (CA) Dismissing the defendant's appeal, that in the circumstances the repeated statement that the money was "as much yours as mine" was sufficient to constitute a declaration of trust in favour of himself and the plaintiff. The judge was correct to award the plaintiff a half share. [1977] 1 W.L.R. 527

COMMENTARY

To create an express trust, the settlor's words and actions must show a clear intention to dispose of the property in such a way that someone else could acquire a beneficial interest. The other half went to his estate and thereafter to the widow, the deceased having died intestate. In *Re Steele's Will Trusts* [1948] Ch. 603 it was held that a valid trust was created where previously judicially approved words were used. In the case there was evidence that the settlor relied on the words of the earlier case to create a valid trust.

KEY PRINCIPLE: *A governmental obligation, though described as a trust, is not enforceable by a court as a fiduciary duty owed to beneficiaries.*

Tito v. Waddell (No. 2) 1977

A series of agreements provided for the mining of phosphates from land in the Gilbert and Ellice Island Colony. The agreements were limited to certain lands. Monies were to be paid to the landowners as well as a royalty to the government. Land that was worked out was to be re-planted and returned to its owners. The mining authorities wished to extend the lands to be mined. The inhabitants opposed this strongly. In 1928 a mining ordinance was enacted authorizing the compulsory acquisition of further land. The land was to be held by the colonial resident commissioner and thus was Crown land. Land was then leased in 1931 with agreement that any compensation or royalty was payable to the resident commissioner "on trust" for the former landowners. A further ordinance in 1937 removed mention of any trust but provided that monies were to be applied as directed by the High Commissioner for the benefit of natives of the island affected. In 1940, and again in 1947, further lands were acquired in return for improved terms. It was believed that the islanders received less than a fair share of the monies obtained. They claimed that the Crown was subject to trust or fiduciary duty for the benefit of the plaintiffs or their pre-decessors.

HELD: (Ch.D.) The use of the word "trust" in relation to the Crown did not necessarily create a trust enforceable by the court. There may have been a governmental obligation not enforceable by the court. [1977] Ch. 106

COMMENTARY

The court described a regular trust as a trust in the lower sense and the type of government obligation seen here as a trust in the higher sense. It may seem ironical that such a "higher trust" is not enforceable by a court. Both as a matter of construction and constitutional law it would be very difficult for a court to enforce a government obligation.

(ii) Certainty of subject matter

KEY PRINCIPLE: *The subject matter of a trust must be identified with certainty.*

Palmer v. Simmonds 1854

A testatrix bequeathed her residuary estate to A. The bequest was phrased to be for his own use and benefit in full confidence if he should die without children, he would, after providing for his widow, leave the bulk of her residuary estate to B, C, D, and E.

HELD: (V.-C.C.) The terms of the bequest did not describe the subject of the gift with sufficient certainty to create a trust. (1854) 2 Drew. 221

COMMENTARY

There was no binding obligation on the inheritor to hold the property on trust during his lifetime. Being for his full use and benefit he could dispose of it as he wished. As in *Comiskey v. Bowring-Hanbury*, there could have been an executory gift but unlike that case there was no way of ascertaining the subject matter of the potential gift. Thus B, C, D and E would not be beneficiaries able to enforce the gift.

KEY PRINCIPLE: *The investment powers relating to the subject matter of a trust must be identified with certainty.*

Re Kolb's Will Trusts 1962

A testator bequeathed his estate to trustees on trust to invest in "such stocks, shares and/or convertible debentures in the blue chip category" as his trustees thought fit but not to invest in British or other government securities or trustee securities or fixed interest stock or debentures. The trustees sought a declaration as to the meaning of the instructions as to investment.

HELD: (Ch.) The term "blue chip" depended on the standards of the testator and was not an objective quality. The testator had not communicated his standard of blue chip to the trustees and thus the investment instructions were void for uncertainty. [1962] Ch. 531

COMMENTARY
Here, the subject-matter was not uncertain but the means of investing it was. The trust was still valid but its investment terms were void for uncertainty. The statutory powers of investment consequently applied.

KEY PRINCIPLE: *An uncertain term as to subject-matter may be valid if there is a means of ascertaining its value.*

Re Golay's Will Trusts 1965

The testator directed that the beneficiary of his will benefit from the use of a flat during her lifetime and "receive a reasonable income from my other properties . . .". The trustee sought a declaration that the direction was void for uncertainty.

HELD: (Ch.) The phrase "reasonable income" was capable of being interpreted. The testator's intention could be given effect. The phrase was not meant to depend on the subjective interpretation of another person. It could be objectively determined by the court. [1965] 1 W.L.R. 969

COMMENTARY
Courts are familiar with making such assessments in family law cases as well as in trust law. The courts are willing to save a term if it is ascertainable even if it has not been pre-defined with exact certainty.

KEY PRINCIPLE: *A residuary sum is not sufficiently certain if it is in the power of the donee to determine its size.*

Sprange v. Barnard 1789

The testatrix left £300 to her husband. The bequest was phrased: "by which she gives it to her husband; but so much as shall be remaining at his death to her brother and sisters."

HELD: (Rolls Court) The £300 vested absolutely in the husband. The property to be left over to the relatives was not sufficiently certain to give rise to a trust. (1789) 2 Bro. C.C. 585

COMMENTARY
This case could easily have been decided on the point that there was inconclusive intent to create a trust. However, the case is decided on the point that there is no certainty of subject matter.

(iii) Certainty of objects

KEY PRINCIPLE: *There must be a beneficiary who can enforce the trust.*

Re Endacott 1960
The testator left his residuary estate to the Parish Council "for the purpose of providing some useful memorial to myself".

HELD: (CA) As a matter of construction the bequest was not a gift but imposed an obligation in the nature of a trust. The trust could not be charitable because the parish's activities were not solely charitable and the gift was not clearly for the benefit of the community in a charitable sense. The gift could not take effect as a non-charitable public trust because its terms were insufficiently certain. [1960] Ch. 232

COMMENTARY
Normally a trust must have known human beneficiaries or a charity as its beneficiary in order to be enforceable. There is an anomalous class of gifts to public bodies which though not charitable can be held to be bound in trust where the bequest is sufficiently precise. This case fell outside the anomalous class. The gift was thus void for lack of a beneficiary. A beneficiary who can enforce, is an essential element of a trust otherwise there would be no enforceable obligation against the holder of the property: *Morice v. Bishop of Durham* (1805) 10 Ves. 522.

KEY PRINCIPLE: *In a discretionary trust it is sufficient that it can be said with certainty whether a given person falls within the class or not.*

McPhail v. Doulton 1971

A settlement was made of shares for the benefit of employees of the company and their relatives and dependants. The trustees had absolute discretion as to how, whether or when they should distribute money from the fund. The executors of the settlor's estate argued that the settlement was void for uncertainty.

HELD: (HL) The settlement created a trust not merely a power. The test for certainty of objects in a discretionary trust was whether it could be said with certainty whether any given individual was or was not a member of the class. [1971] A.C. 424

COMMENTARY

[1] In a fixed trust, all beneficiaries must be ascertained or ascertainable.

[2] In *McPhail v. Doulton*, the formulation for the test of certainty for a discretionary trust was in fact taken from the test set out for powers in *Re Gulbenkian's Settlement*, below. The logic behind the new test was that a trustee could discharge his duty within the terms of his discretion without necessarily knowing at any one time who all the potential beneficiaries were. This is illustrated by the terms of the discretion here, where it was not intended that the trustees should use up the fund's income in any one year but could hold back money till the need arose. Equally, if a significant need arose then capital could be used from the fund.

KEY PRINCIPLE: *In applying the test in McPhail v. Doulton the court should look to the conceptual certainty of the description of the class.*

Re Baden's Deed Trusts (No. 2) 1973

The House of Lords in *McPhail v. Doulton* remitted the case back to the Chancery Division in order to apply the test as now set out.

HELD: (CA) Affirming the application of the test by the Chancery Division the court said it was necessary to distinguish between conceptual certainty and evdential difficulty. The terms "relatives" and "dependants" were not conceptually uncertain. They could each be given the widest meaning attributable which would avoid uncertainty. Relatives could be interpreted as meaning "all descendants of a common ancestor" which would be sufficiently conceptually certain for a person to be identified as being within that class or not. [1973] Ch. 9

COMMENTARY

That it may be evidentially difficult for an individual to prove his ancestry was not the issue. The issue was whether a court could find sufficient conceptual certainty in the terms used, against which a person could be tested as to whether he came within the class or not. In *Re Tuck's Settlement Trusts* [1978] Ch. 49, the phrase "an approved wife" was regarded as conceptually certain as it was qualified by the term "of Jewish blood by one or both of her parents". This latter term could itself be subject to ascertainment by the Chief Rabbi. In *Re Barlow's Will Trusts* [1979] 1 W.L.R. 278, it was held that the terms "family" and "friends" were sufficiently certain.This could be explained on the basis that the case concerned a gift subject to a condition precedent. In these cases the courts have shown a preference for holding a trust or gift valid.

KEY PRINCIPLE: *A power of appointment is valid if it can be said with certainty whether a person was within the class or not.*

Re Gulbenkian's Settlement 1970

The question arose as to whether powers of appointment were void for uncertainty. The potential appointees were described as "all or any one or more to the exclusion of the other or others of the following persons, namely . . . and any wife and his children or remoter issue for the time being in existence whether minors or adults and any person or persons in whose house or apartments or in whose company or under whose care or control or by or with whom . . . may from time to time be employed or residing . . .".

HELD: (HL) Provided there was a valid gift over in default of appointment, a power of appointment was valid if it could be said with certainty whether a person was a member of the class or not. Where the language was ambiguous it was the court's duty to seek to ascertain the settlor's intentions. That the court had to disentangle the language, did not of itself mean the power was uncertain. [1970] A.C. 508

COMMENTARY
The court's emphasis is on giving effect to the settlor's intent to allow the power to be exercised with discretion. In *Re Manisty's Settlement* [1974] 1 Ch. 17, the trustees were empowered at their absolute discretion to add anyone to the class of beneficiaries other than an excepted class. The excepted class was sufficiently certain to in turn make anyone other than part of the excepted class sufficiently certain. The apparent breadth of the class may have been regarded as inconsistent with the nature of a power. The court, however, took the view that the exercise was certain and had been allowed for by the settlor. Similarly, in *Re Hay's Settlement Trusts* [1982] 1 W.L.R. 202, a power to appoint anyone apart from a small number of specified persons was conceptually certain and administratively workable. It is generally thought that the test of administrative unworkability applies to discretionary trusts but not powers: *R. v. District Auditor ex parte West Yorkshire Metropolitan County Council* [1985] 26 R.V.R. 24. Where the power is exercised by a fiduciary, then administrative unworkability may be a way of determining validity of the power: *Mettoy Pension Trustees Ltd v. Evans* [1991] 1 W.L.R. 1587.

[B] FORMALITIES

KEY PRINCIPLE: *It is a fraud for a person to whom land is conveyed as trustee, and who knows it was so conveyed, to deny the trust and claim the land as his own.*

Hodgson v. Marks 1971
(See Chap. 7).

HELD: (CA) The failure to satisfy the requirements in section 53(1) of the *Law of Property Act 1925* to create an express trust of land in favour of the donor does not prevent the existence of a resulting trust back to the donor. [1971] Ch. 892

COMMENTARY
The requirement of evidence in writing of a declaration of trust does not mean that other evidence of a trust cannot be

adduced where the absence of writing is being used to deny the nature of the transaction. The case embodies the equitable maxim that equity will not allow a statute to be used an instrument of fraud.

KEY PRINCIPLE: *A disposition of a legal and equitable interest of personalty together need not be in writing but the disposition must be complete, otherwise there may be a resulting trust back to the settlor.*

Vandervell v. Inland Revenue Commissioners 1967

In 1958, Vandervell decided to make a gift of £150,000 to the Royal College of Surgeons to endow a Chair of pharmacology. At the time 100,000 shares in Vandervell Products Ltd, (VPL), a company which he controlled, were held by a bank on trust. It was decided that the shares should be transferred to the college and that an option to buy them should be granted to a trustee company and that sufficient dividends to pay for the endowment should be declared on the shares. The trustee company's principal activity was to act as trustee of settlements made in favour of Vandervell's children. On November 19, the transfer deed of the 100,000 shares was executed by the bank which was sealed by the college the next day along with the option deed. Dividends were declared on the shares. In 1961, the trustee company exercised its option to buy back the shares for £5,000. Vandervell was assessed for surtax on the dividends paid on the basis that the transaction amounted to a settlement of property of which he had not absolutely divested himself. It was argued that Vandervell had not divested himself of the beneficial interest in the shares because there had been no written disposition within the meaning of section 53(1)(c) of the *Law of Property Act 1925*.

HELD: (HL) Section 53(1)(c) was inapplicable as it applied to situations where the beneficial interest was divided from the legal interest and was designed to prevent secret, fraudulent dealings behind the legal owners back. Where, as here, the beneficial owner directed the bare trustee (the Bank) to deal with both the legal and beneficial interest (transferring them to the college) there was no need to satisfy section 53(1)(c). The option, however, was vested in the trustee on trusts not defined.

There was a resulting trust back to Vandervell of the benefit of the option. He had not divested himself of the shares and was liable to surtax for them. [1967] 2 A.C. 291

COMMENTARY
The decision is questionable. As the shares were being moved from being used as security for a trust to Vandervell's wife to a beneficial interest for the college, this would seem to be a disposition of a beneficial interest. Vandervell had set up a clever scheme to transfer shares to the college whereby as owner of the company he could control the amount of dividends payable and as owner of the option at an undervalue he would recover control over the shares. In a commercial sense he had not divested himself of his interest in the shares, but the court's reasoning behind his retention of an interest is not convincing.

KEY PRINCIPLE: *An oral declaration of a disposition of an equitable interest is ineffective to transfer the interest for the purposes of section 53(1)(c) of the Law of Property Act 1925.*

Grey v. Inland Revenue Commissioners 1960

In 1949, H made a settlement for each of his five grandchildren and a sixth for existing and afterborn grandchildren. On February 1, 1955, he transferred 18,000 shares to the trustees of the settlements as nominees. On February 18, 1955, he orally directed the trustees to hold the shares in blocks of 3,000 for each of the settlements with the intent of divesting himself of any interest in the shares. On March 25, 1955, the trustees executed declarations of trust of the shares; H, though not expressed to be a party thereto executed the declarations. The declarations recited H's oral direction of February 18. The transfers of the shares were assessed for stamp duty.

HELD: (HL) The directions of February 18 were dispositions of the equitable interest in the shares within the meaning of section 53(1)(c). As they were not in writing, they were not effective for that purpose. However, the declarations of March 25 were effective as dispositions of his equitable interest and were assessable for stamp duty. [1960] 1 A.C. 1

COMMENTARY
The substance of the arrangement was a transfer of the beneficial interest in shares from the settlor to the children. A direction by a beneficiary to settlors that a benefit should be held for third parties is a disposition of an equitable interest which had to be in writing. A declaration of oneself as trustee of a beneficial interest under a trust does not amount to a disposition of an equitable interest if as intermediate trustee active duties are retained. If the property is held as a bare trustee then this may be a disposition. See *Grainge v. Wilberforce* (1889) 5 T.L.R. 436

KEY PRINCIPLE: *A specifically enforceable contract could make the transferor a constructive trustee of property to hold for the transferee who thereby acquired an equitable interest.*

Oughtred v. Inland Revenue Commissioners 1960

Under a settlement made in 1924, a mother had a life interest in 100,000 preference shares and 100,000 ordinary shares in a company. Her son was the owner of the shares subject to the mother's life interest. By an oral agreement on June 18, 1956, it was agreed that he would transfer his interest in the shares intending to give her absolute title to them. This was in return for her transferring 72,000 shares to him. By a deed on June 26, 1956, the mother and son released the trustees and stated that the shares were held in trust for the mother absolutely. The transfer was expressed to be in consideration for the release. On the same day a deed was made by the trustees and the mother transferring the shares to her for consideration of 10 shillings.

HELD: (HL) The transfer was assessable for *ad valorem* stamp duty, being an instrument whereby the property (the settled shares) was transferred by sale to the mother. By the transfer, the mother acquired the reversionary interest as if it had been transferred direct from the son. [1960] A.C. 206

Neville v. Wilson 1996

JE Ltd, a small family company was the registered owner of all but 120 of the issued shares in UE Ltd. The 120 shares were in the names of two directors of UE Ltd as nominees for JE Ltd.

In 1965 it was resolved to transfer all the registered shares held by JE Ltd to the shareholders of JE Ltd in proportion to their shareholding. This did not extend to the 120 shares. From 1969 onwards, JE Ltd was regarded as having been defunct and was dissolved. The issue arose as to the beneficial ownership of the 120 shares in UE Ltd. The plaintiffs, who were two share-holders of JE Ltd, claimed that the shares were held on a constructive trust for the shareholders in proportions corre-sponding to their shareholdings in that company. At first instance, the judge ruled that the 1965 resolution did not extend to the 120 shares. The plaintiffs appealed, raising an alternative claim that there was an agreement in 1969 between the shareholders of JE Ltd for the informal liquidation of the company. Under this, the debts and liabilities of the company were to be discharged and the balance of the assets distributed to the shareholders in proportion to their shareholding. This included the beneficial interest in the 120 shares. The issue arose as to whether if such an agreement existed, the require-ments of section 53(1)(c) of the *Law of Property Act 1925* would render the agreement ineffective for lack of writing.

HELD: (CA) Section 53(1)(c) of the *Law of Property Act 1925* did not render such an agreement ineffective. The effect of the agreement between the shareholders as to the disposal of the assets of the company gave rise to a constructive trust between them which in accordance with section 53(2) of the *Law of Property Act 1925*, did not require compliance with section 53(1)(c) of the *Law of Property Act 1925*. The beneficial interest in the 120 shares was vested in the shareholders JE Ltd in proportion to their shareholding and not in the Crown as *bona vacantia*. [1996] 3 All E.R. 171

COMMENTARY

In *Oughtred v. I.R.C.*, the oral agreement of June 18 was a specifically enforceable contract. At that point, the son became a constructive trustee of the equitable reversionary interest. It was said that section 53(1)(c) does not apply to constructive trusts (which is true) and thus the transfer to the mother of the interest was complete without writing and that the subsequent deeds of transfer were confirmatory of the transfer rather than the actual transfer itself. The court found that notwithstanding the constructive trust, the transfer in writing did pass some beneficial interest in the shares which attracted ad valorem stamp duty. The case of *Neville v. Wilson* is a good illustration of the application of section 53(2).

KEY PRINCIPLE: *A declaration of trusts of personalty does not require compliance with section 53 of the Law of Property Act 1925.*

Re Vandervell's Trusts (No. 2) 1974

(See *Vandervell v. I.R.C.*, above).

In 1949, Vandervell had set up trusts for his children. Vandervell Trustees Ltd was the trustee. Vandervell intended that the trustee held the option on unspecified trusts for the children or his employees. It was this option in *Vandervell v. I.R.C.* which the court held returned to him on resulting trust because he could not be said to have divested himself of his interest. Having been held liable to surtax, Vandervell by deed of January 19, 1965, transferred all his rights in the option to the trust company, the shares to be held on the trusts of the children's settlement. Vandervell died in 1967. The Inland Revenue assessed his estate to £628,229 in respect of the dividends from 1961 to 1965, *i.e.* from the exercise of the option till the deed of divestment. The plaintiffs, who were executors of the estate, brought this action against the trustees for a declaration that the estate was entitled to all moneys received by the trustee as dividends between 1961 and 1965. This was on the basis that as Vandervell had not divested himself of all interest in the shares, he should be entitled to the dividends on them. They also contended that the option of the beneficial interest in the shares could not be held on the trusts of the children's settlement because there had been no disposition within section 53(1)(c) of the *Law of Property Act 1925*.

HELD: (CA) Until 1961, the trustee held the option on such trust as might thereafter be declared by the trustee or Vandervell. As no clear trusts had been declared there was a resulting trust to Vandervell. In the exercise of the option, £5,000 was used from the children's settlement, the trustee held the 100,000 shares on trust for the children as indicated by the trustee's and Vandervell's intention. Neither the extinction of the option after its exercise, nor the declaration of trust

amounted to disposition of an equitable interest within section
53(1)(c). [1974] Ch. 269

COMMENTARY
Having been caught in *Vandervell v. I.R.C.*, above, for not
ensuring that the declaration of trust of the option divested
himself of all interest in the shares, Vandervell's estate is now
told that he had no interest in value of the dividends on the
shares because the declaration of trust for the children didn't
have to be in writing. Whilst there was sympathy for Vandervell because of the court's reasoning and because he was
paying tax at up to a rate of 95 per cent, he might have been
better off keeping things simple.

KEY PRINCIPLE: *Section 53(1)(c) of the Law of Property Act
1925 should not apply to a right of nomination of a beneficiary
under a staff pension fund.*

Re Danish Bacon Co. Ltd Staff Pension Fund Trusts 1971
The question arose as to whether the appointment of or subsequent replacement of a nominee to receive benefits under a
staff pension scheme required compliance with any formalities.

HELD: (Ch.) Although the appointment had some testamentary characteristics it was not a testamentary paper and there
were no special formalities required for nomination of a pension beneficiary. Even if section 53(1)(c) applied, the original
form of appointment which complied with the fund's rules and
the subsequent letter as acted upon by the trustee would be a
sufficient connection of documents to satisfy the requirements
of writing. [1971] 1 W.L.R. 248

[C] CONSTITUTION OF TRUSTS

KEY PRINCIPLE: *The appropriate mode of vesting property
in a trustee must be used.*

Milroy v. Lord 1862
S attempted to transfer shares to SL by a voluntary deed.
Shares can only be transferred fully by registering the new
owner of the shares with the company. This was not done.

HELD: (CA) The transfer of shares was not effective. Moreover, the court dismissed the claim that a failed transfer could constitute a declaration of trust. (1862) 4 De. G.F. & J. 264

COMMENTARY
The formalities for the transfer of other kinds of property include:

(a) a transfer of a legal estate in land must by deed: section 52(1) of the *Law of Property Act 1925*;
(b) a disposition of a subsisting equitable interest must be in writing: section 53(1)(c) of the *Law of Property Act 1925*;
(c) a legal assignment of a chose in action should come within section 136 of the *Law of Property Act 1925*;
(d) a transfer of shares must come within section 183 of the *Companies Act 1985*;
(e) a transfer of personalty can be done by delivery or deed of gift.

KEY PRINCIPLE: *Equity will not perfect an imperfect gift.*

Jones v. Lock 1865
(See Chap. 1).

HELD: (CA) There had not been a transfer of the property as it had not been delivered. It could not be construed as a declaration of trust either. (1865) L.R. 1 Ch. 4

COMMENTARY
As in *Milroy v. Lord*, a failed transfer cannot be treated on default as a declaration of trust because, without clear evidence, the attempt could inferred to be a an outright gift as much as a trust. The courts do on occasion recognise a declaration of trust where it is clearly evidenced by the facts as in *Paul v. Constance*, above.

KEY PRINCIPLE: *Where the transferor has done all in his power to complete the transfer the transfer will be given effect in equity.*

Re Rose 1952

The deceased had transferred 10,000 shares in a company to his wife on March 30, 1943. On the same day, he transferred another 10,000 shares in the same company to trustees to hold on trust. The transfers were done in the form required by the company's articles of association. These allowed the directors to reject any transfer. On the date of execution, the transfers and share certificates were handed to the transferees. These were duly stamped and registered on April 12, 1943, and registered in the books of the company on June 30, 1943. The deceased died in 1947. The Crown claimed estate duty on the ground that the gift was not completed by April 10, 1943 (the relevant date for completion of transfer to avoid the tax).

HELD: (CA) The deceased had done everything in his power to transfer the legal and beneficial interest in the shares. By the execution the transferees had become beneficial owners of the shares and he had ceded (notwithstanding that he was still registered owner) any claim to a beneficial interest in them. Having regard to the nature of the property and its mode of transfer as well as the directors' ability to hold up registration, the transferor was in a position of trustee. The beneficial interest in the shares passed bona fide on March 30, 1943, and consequently was not assessable for estate duty. [1952] Ch. 499

COMMENTARY

In *Re Fry* [1946] Ch. 312, the court took a much stricter view. Fry owned shares in an English company. He made a voluntary transfer of these. He sent the transfer papers to the transferees who passed them onto the company for registration. Under wartime regulations the consent of the Treasury had to be obtained. Before it was obtained he died. It was held that the intended gift failed as it was not complete and that the property should revert to his estate. It was said that he had not done all within his powers to transfer the shares because the Treasury could have requested further details from him before giving consent.

KEY PRINCIPLE: *Where transferees have provided consideration they may seek specific performance to complete the transfer of property.*

Pullan v. Koe 1913

By a marriage settlement it was provided that the wife would settle any after-acquired property exceeding £100 in value. She received £3,285 from her mother which she put in her husband's bank account. This money was later used by the husband to buy securities. On his death the trustees claimed the securities from the estate.

HELD: (Ch.) The securities were not part of the estate but were part of the trusts of the marriage settlement, the beneficiaries of which were the children. The children could seek specific performance to ensure that the securities were part of their trust rather than the father's estate because they were deemed to be part of the consideration in the marriage settlement. [1913] 1 Ch. 9

COMMENTARY

They could proceed in equity notwithstanding that an action in common law was time barred. The requirement of consideration is a straightforward common law principle but was being given effect through equity to enforce a trust.

KEY PRINCIPLE: *Equity will not assist a volunteer to enforce a trust.*

Re Plumptre's Marriage Settlement 1910

Upon marriage, the husband and wife covenanted with the trustees that the wife's after-acquired property would be settled on trust for the husband and wife successively for life thereafter to the children, if any, and thereafter to the next of kin. The husband bought shares in the wife's name which she sold and bought other shares with the proceeds. In 1909, the shares were worth £1,125. The wife died childless. The trustees sought a ruling as to whether the property was bound to the trusts of the settlement or whether they should seek to secure the transfer of the property given that the next of kin were volunteers.

HELD: (Ch.) The next of kin were volunteers being strangers to the marriage consideration. They could not enforce the covenant against the husband. [1910] 1 Ch. 609

COMMENTARY

The question in many of these cases is whether property which should go into the trusts of the settlement should be recovered. Otherwise it will fall into the hands of undeserving volunteers. If the trustees stay passive its ownership will remain with the individual who can deal with it more freely. The justification for not forcing the trustees to act is the maxim that equity will not assist a volunteer. The courts can use this approach because as the property had not been transferred into the settlement yet, the trust was not fully constituted.

KEY PRINCIPLE: *The court will not indirectly assist volunteers to enforce a covenant which they could not enforce by direct means themselves.*

Re Pryce 1917

A marriage settlement contained a covenant to settle the wife's after-acquired property on the trusts of the settlement. The husband made a gift of certain reversionary interests to which he would be entitled when his mother died. He pre-deceased his mother. His wife was entitled to a life interest in the marriage settlement's property, thereafter the property went to the children, if any, and then to the next of kin. The reversionary interest was bound up in another settlement. The question arose as to whether the trustees should seek to enforce the transfer of the property to the settlement.

HELD: (Ch.) The property should be part of the settlement but the trustees need not enforce it as the next of kin, who were ultimately entitled, were volunteers. The trustees ought not take any steps to assist the volunteers. [1917] 1 Ch. 234

COMMENTARY

[1] Volunteers by not providing consideration could not sue in common law for damages for breach of covenant to settle property. If trustees were to do this, or sue in equity for specific performance of the promise, then the volunteers would be in a better position that they would be on their own.

[2] In *Re Kay's Settlement* [1939] Ch. 329, it was held that the trustees should not pursue specific performance but that they should also not take proceedings at common law for breach of covenant. This approach was also taken in *Re Cook's Settlement Trusts* [1965] Ch. 902. The approach was, however, departed from in *Re Cavendish Browne's Settlement Trust* (1916) W.N. 341 where the court allowed the trustees to sue for and obtain damages for breach of covenant.

KEY PRINCIPLE: *The concept of a trust of the benefit of a covenant can be used to enable a beneficiary to sue upon a trust.*

Fletcher v. Fletcher 1844

Fletcher covenanted with trustees, for himself, his heirs, executors and administrators to pay the trustees £60,000 within 12 months of death to be held on trust for his sons, John and Jacob. If both sons were alive at his death and attained the age of 21, the money was to be held on trust for them in equal shares as tenants in common. John survived his father but died before reaching 21. Jacob claimed the full amount. The trustees refused to accept the money or take proceedings to claim it without the direction of the court.

HELD: (V.-C.C.) Jacob could claim the full amount direct from the executors. The trust was perfect in the sense that the covenantor had incurred liability in law because the covenant by deed could be enforced at law. Equity would allow Jacob to stand in place of the trustees to sue or he could sue in his own name at law. (1844) 4 Hare. 67

COMMENTARY
[1] The trust was not fully constituted in the conventional sense in that the £60,000 had not been transferred to the trust. The trustees would not have sought to force constitution of the trust as this would assist a volunteer. However, in the present case it was interpreted that there was a trust of the benefit of the covenant which was itself constituted by the covenant made to the trustees. If this is the case it might seem simpler for the trustee to sue at common law. However, the beneficiary could not compel the trustee to do so unless there was deemed to be a trust of the benefit in which case

the beneficiary could sue anyway. The difficulty in most of these cases would be ascertaining the requisite intention to create the trust of the benefit of the covenant.

[2] Where the trust is of future property, it would seem that the volunteer beneficiary could not enforce at all: *Re Ellenborough* [1903] 1 Ch. 697. Conversely, where the beneficiary is party to the deed then he may sue for damages at common law even when a volunteer: *Cannon v. Hartley* [1949] 1 All E.R. 50.

KEY PRINCIPLE: *The rule in Strong v. Bird serves as an exception to the rule that equity will not assist a volunteer.*

Strong v. Bird 1874

Bird borrowed £1,100 from his stepmother who lived in his house paying £212.10s per quarter. It was agreed that the loan should be paid off by her deducting £100 from each quarter's rent. This was done twice but thereafter the stepmother refused to make the deduction and paid the full charge until her death four years later. Bird was appointed sole executor of the estate. The next of kin claimed that Bird owed the estate £900.

HELD: (Ch.) The appointment as executor relieved him of the debt. [1874] L.R. 17 Eq. 315

COMMENTARY

Where a person owing a debt is made executor he is released from the debt provided that there was a clear ongoing intention to forgive the debt. If this is the case the volunteer who is forgiven the debt for no consideration will be assisted by equity. This is a convenient result given that it would be difficult for the executor to sue himself. See also *Re Ralli's Will Trusts* [1964] Ch. 288.

KEY PRINCIPLE: *The principle of* donatio mortis causa *serves, as an exception to the rule that equity will not assist a volunteer.*

Woodard v. Woodard 1995

A father who was dying from leukaemia, told the defendant that he could keep the keys to his car as he (the father) would not be driving it anymore. This was in the plaintiff's presence. The father died three days later. The plaintiff claimed the proceeds of the sale of the car which amounted to £3,900. The defendant argued that the father either made an outright gift or a *donatio mortis causa* (DMC) of the car.

HELD: (CA) From the evidence, it was clear that the defendant would have to return the car on the father's recovery. There was, therefore, no outright gift of the car. However, the gift had been made in contemplation of death and on condition that the gift was to be made absolute on the father's death. It was irrelevant that the defendant already had possession of the car and the set of keys. There was a valid DMC of the car. [1995] 3 All E.R. 980

COMMENTARY

[1] A gift made *inter vivos* can take effect if the three essentials laid down by Lord Russell in *Cain v. Moon* [1896] 2 Q.B. 283, are satisfied:

  (a) the gift must have been made in contemplation, though not necessarily in expectation, of death;
  (b) the subject matter of the gift must have been delivered to the donee;
  (c) the gift must have been made under such circumstances to show that the property is to revert to the donor if he should recover.

[2] The rule allows a volunteer to take a gift of property which would otherwise go into the deceased's estate. Certain types of property are excluded from the rule including, stocks, and cheques. There is still some doubt as to whether land can be the subject matter of a DMC (see *Sen v. Headley* [1991] Ch. 425).

5. SECRET AND PROTECTIVE TRUSTS

[A] SECRET TRUSTS

Fully Secret Trusts

KEY PRINCIPLE: *The trust must be communicated to the secret trustee before the testator's death.*

Wallgrave v. Tebbs 1855

Property was left to the defendants as joint tenants. The action was brought to declare the transfer void on the basis that the transfer had been made upon trust for the defendants to carry out certain charitable purposes intended by the testator. It was alleged that the defendants knew of this intention and that a letter setting this out had been drafted, albeit never signed. The defendants denied that they had any communication with the testator about his will.

HELD: (V.-C.C.) There was no evidence of understanding between the testator and the defendants; there was no communication between them which could be construed as a trust to give effect to the testator's intent. The transfer to the defendants was valid. They held the property absolutely for their own purposes. (1855) 2 K. & J. 313

COMMENTARY
A person cannot be bound by an obligation unless it is communicated to him. This must be before the death of the testator because it is from that point that the trustee will be bound. If a trustee did not wish to be bound he must communicate this to the testator. It does not matter whether the communication is made before or after the will has been made: *Moss v. Cooper* (1861) 1 S. & H. 352. This was applied in *Re Gardner* [1920] 2 Ch. 523 where a wife left her estate to her husband "knowing he will carry out my wishes". On the evidence it was found that she had communicated those

wishes to her husband after the will. There was a valid secret trust.

KEY PRINCIPLE: *The terms of the trust must be communicated to the secret trustee.*

Re Boyes 1884

A testator instructed his solicitor to draft a will leaving all his property to the solicitor absolutely, but to be held by him and distributed according to instructions which were to be subsequently given to him. The will was so drafted but no further instructions were given to the solicitor during the testator's lifetime. After the testator's death, an unattested paper was found indicating the testator's wish that the property should be given to X and Y with a small amount for the solicitor. The solicitor accepting this agreed to hold all but his indicated share on trust for X and Y.

HELD: (Ch.) The terms of the trust were not communicated during the testator's lifetime. No valid trust was created in favour of X and Y. The solicitor held the property on resulting trust for the estate with the consequence that it would go to the next of kin. (1884) 26 Ch. D. 531

COMMENTARY

[1] This result is what the testator precisely wanted to avoid. It is possible for the terms to be constructively communicated by way of a sealed letter: *Re Keen* [1937] Ch. 236. This may make sense in preventing the secret trustee committing a fraud by taking the property absolutely but does not afford the trustee the opportunity to decline the obligation.

[2] Where a trust is communicated to one secret trustee but not the other, whether both are bound depends on whether they take the property as joint tenants or tenants in common. If they take as tenants in common, only the person to whom the communication was made is bound. Where the property is taken as joint tenants, it depends on whether the communication is made before the will is made or after. If before, both trustees are bound on the basis that there would be a suspicion that the testator would be fraudulently induced into executing the will which would otherwise not bind the other trustee and would take the whole property beneficially. If after, then only the trustee to whom communication was made

would be bound as there would be no suspicion of inducement: *Re Stead* [1900] 1 Ch. 237.

KEY PRINCIPLE: *A legal obligation as opposed to just a moral obligation must be imposed on the secret trustee.*

McCormick v. Grogan 1868

A testator left all his property to the defendant. He later fell ill with cholera. On his deathbed he told the defendant that his will and a letter were in his desk. The letter set out his intended beneficiaries and bequests. The testator concluded the letter saying that he did not expect the defendant to carry out the instructions strictly, but to use his judgement as he thought the testator would use his as to which of the parties were deserving. The defendant excluded one of the possible beneficiaries, an illegitimate child, who subsequently sued.

HELD: (HL) There was no valid secret trust. The letter imported a moral obligation as opposed to a legal one. (1869) L.R. 4 H.L. 82

Re Snowden 1979

A testatrix left the residue of her estate to her brother with whom she had lived for the last six months of her life. He died six days after the testatrix leaving his son as sole beneficiary of his will. Nineteen relatives challenged the testatrix's will claiming that the brother had received the legacy on secret trust for them. There was a solicitor's note indicating that she meant to leave legacies to her relatives, leaving the brother to split up the remainder of the estate.

HELD: (Ch.) The standard of proof for establishing a secret trust was the same ordinary civil standard of proof. There was insufficient evidence to show that the testatrix intended to bind the brother by a legally enforceable trust. There was a moral obligation on him to distribute as she would have done. Consequently, the brother and his son thereafter took the residue absolutely. [1979] Ch. 528

COMMENTARY
The whole point of a trust, secret or otherwise, is that it affixes to the trustee a legal obligation going beyond a moral one. See Chap. 4.

KEY PRINCIPLE: *The legal obligation must be accepted by the secret trustee.*

Ottoway v. Norman 1972
H bequeathed his house and its contents to E . He intended that she would leave his house to his son. Shortly before her death, however, she made a new will leaving the property to the defendant and his wife. She left her residuary estate, half to the plaintiff and half to the defendant. The plaintiffs (who were the son and his wife) claimed that the house, contents and E's residuary estate should have gone to them.

HELD: (Ch.) The plaintiffs established that there was a secret trust of the house in their favour and such of its contents which passed in the will from H to E. There was insufficient evidence of a secret trust of the remaining contents or the residuary estate. To establish that a secret trust had been created one had to show that the testator intended to impose an obligation upon the first donee and that such intention was communicated to the first donee who accepted the obligation. It was not necessary to show any wrongdoing by the donee as the trust was established at the outset. [1972] Ch. 698

COMMENTARY
Acceptance of the obligations of a secret trustee can be express, implied (*Wallgrave v. Tebbs*, above) or by acquiescence (*Moss v. Cooper, above).*

Half Secret Trusts

KEY PRINCIPLE: *The trust must be communicated to the half-secret trustee before the testator's will is made.*

Blackwell v. Blackwell 1929
A testator by a codicil gave five persons £12,000 upon trust to invest as they thought fit and to apply the income "for the purposes indicated by me to them" with a power to pay a sum of £8,000 ". . . to such person or persons indicated by

me to them" as they thought fit. Detailed parol instructions were given by the testator to C, one of the trustees. The object and outline was known and accepted by all five before the codicil was executed. On the same day, soon after the codicil was executed, C wrote out and signed a memorandum of the detailed instructions. The income was to be applied for the benefit of a lady and her son. The widow and her son brought an action to test the validity of the legacy.

HELD: (HL) Parol evidence was admissible to establish a trust. A valid and consistent trust had been created by the codicil and memorandum on the same day. [1929] A.C. 318

Re Bateman's Will Trusts 1970

A testator directed his trustees to set aside £24,000 from his estate to pay the income thereof "to such persons and in such proportions as shall be stated by me in a sealed letter in my own handwriting addressed to my trustees".

HELD: (Ch.) The direction relating to the sealed letter could not be read as referring only to a past letter but clearly envisaged that the testator might give the trustees a letter at some point in the future. The direction was therefore invalid as an attempt to dispose of the estate by a non-testamentary instrument. The subsequent directions as to the giftover of the £24,000 were likewise invalid. [1970] 1 W.L.R. 817

COMMENTARY

The requirement for the communication of a half-secret trust before the will is executed appears to be inconsistent with the rule in relation to fully secret trusts that it is sufficient for the communication to be made before the testator's death.

Other Issues

KEY PRINCIPLE: *The beneficiary under a secret trust can claim the interest under the trust even though he or she was a witness to the will.*

Re Young 1951

The testator gave a bequest to his wife with a direction for her to make small legacies in accordance with his wishes. Prior to the execution of the will, the testator told his wife that he wished his chauffer to receive a sum of £2,000. The chauffer was one of the witnesses to the will.

HELD: (Ch.) The chauffer was entitled to take the legacy as the secret trust operated outside the *Wills Act 1837*. [1951] Ch. 344

COMMENTARY

[1] Under section 15 of the *Wills Act 1837*, a witness to a will cannot take a benefit under the will. In the present case, the chauffer was allowed to take the legacy because of the principle that the secret trust operated outside (or dehors) the will and therefore did not infringe section 15 of the *Wills Act 1837*. [2] Where the attestation of the will is by the secret trustee, the difficulty in the case of a fully secret trust is that there is no reference on the face of the will to the existence of the trust and therefore section 15 of the *Wills Act 1837* may apply preventing the trustee from taking under the will. In the case of a half secret trust as it is apparent on the face of the will that the secret trustee is taking as a trustee, it is argued that section 15 would not apply. See by analogy *Creswell v. Creswell* (1868) L.R. 6 E.Q. 69.

KEY PRINCIPLE: *Where the beneficiary under a secret trust predeceases the testator, his estate may nonetheless benefit under the trust.*

Re Gardner (No. 2) 1923

A testatrix left her estate to her husband stating that he would carry out her wishes. The testatrix wished the estate to be divided on her husband's death between three beneficiaries, one of whom had predeceased the testatrix.

HELD: (Ch.) The beneficiary's personal representative could claim on behalf of the deceased beneficiary under the secret trust. [1923] 2 Ch. 230

COMMENTARY

The normal rule of succession is that a beneficiary under a will must survive the testator. However, in this case, the court's view was that as the secret trust existed outside the will, the fact the beneficiary predeceased the testatrix did not matter. The court decided that a secret beneficiary becomes entitled upon the creation of the secret trust not on the death of the testatrix. This is unsatisfactory as it ignores the fact that will could be changed by the testatrix at any time prior to the death and could terminate the trust.

KEY PRINCIPLE: *Unless there is clear evidence, the secret trustee cannot take a beneficial interest under the secret trust.*

Re Rees 1950
A testator died and appointed a friend and a solicitor as his executors and trustees, stating that they knew his wishes as regards the property. The testator had told them to make certain payments but to keep the remainder for themselves. There was a surplus after these payments were made. The executors argued that they were entitled to keep the surplus.

HELD: (CA) The executors could not keep the surplus as a fiduciary obligation had been imposed on them. Evidence of the testator's intention was inadmissible as the will clearly showed an intention to create a trust and therefore evidence that the executors were to take the remainder of the property absolutely would contradict the will. [1950] Ch. 204

COMMENTARY
The court suggested that since one of the executors was a solicitor he should have ensured that the will was drafted in a manner which made it clear on the face of the will that the executors could take a benefit under the will rather than by use of a secret trust. See also *Re Pugh's Will Trusts* [1967] 1 W.L.R. 1262.

[B] PROTECTIVE TRUSTS

KEY PRINCIPLE: *The life interest will determine on the principal beneficiary's bankruptcy or where an attempt is made to alienate his interest.*

Re Balfour's Settlement 1938
At the life tenant's request, the trustees advanced capital moneys to him in breach of trust. In order to replace the trust funds, the trustees impounded his beneficial interest. The life tenant subsequently became bankrupt.

HELD: (Ch.) The life's tenant interest had been determined when the beneficial interest had been impounded by the trustees. The life tenant's interest was therefore saved from the bankruptcy. [1938] Ch. 928

Re Dennis's Settlements Trusts 1942
The settlor's son had a protective life interest under a settlement. Upon attaining 21, a rearrangement of the settlement occurred. This provided that the trustees would only pay part of his income and accumulate the rest for the following six years.

HELD: (Ch.) The effect of the rearrangement was to vest the right to receive part of the income on some other person. Accordingly, it brought the forfeiture clause into operation. [1942] Ch. 283

COMMENTARY
Other examples of determining events include a sequestration order (*Re Baring's Settlement Trusts* [1940] Ch. 737) and a court order to pay maintenance to the principal beneficiary's wife on the security of his life interest in the trust and to execute a deed to this effect (*Re Richardson's Will Trusts* [1958] 1 Ch 504). However, in *General Accident, Fire and Life Assurance Corp. Ltd v. I.R.C.* [1963] 1 W.L.R. 1207, a court order which diverted part of the income from a life tenant in favour of his wife on their divorce did not result in forfeiture. The court in that case was of the view that it was not the type of event which the settlor would have intended to be a determining event.

KEY PRINCIPLE: *The effect of legislation can be a determining event.*

Re Gorju's Will Trusts 1943
The principal beneficiary under a protective trust was resident in France. This was under German occupation during the Second World War. The issue was whether the *Trading With the Enemy Act 1939* and the *Trading with the Enemy (Specified Areas) Order* 1940, which provided that persons living in enemy occupied territory would not be entitled to income from Britain, would result in the forfeiture of the principal beneficiary's interest.

HELD: (Ch.) Upon the coming into force of the Act and Order, an event occurred which deprived the principal beneficiary of her income under the protective trust. The property was thereafter held on a discretionary trust in accordance with section 33 of the *Trustee Act 1925*. [1943] 1 Ch. 24

COMMENTARY
The trustees were also prevented from retaining the income for the principal beneficiary until the end of the war. However, in *Re Hall* [1944] Ch. 46, the beneficiary's interest had not been determined by residence in enemy occupied territory. The reason was that the wording used in the instrument as amounting to a determining event restricted it to where the income was payable elsewhere as a result of what she did or suffer any act to be done. As her residence in enemy occupied territory was not as a result of anything she did or allowed to be done, there was no forfeiture.

KEY PRINCIPLE: *The settlor is not permitted to settle his own property on a protective trust on himself until bankruptcy but could do so on the occurrence of other events.*

Re Detmold 1889
S, by his marriage settlement, settled property on trust to pay the income to himself for life, or until he should become bankrupt or shall assign, charge or encumber the life interest, or the occurrence of an event whereby the income would be payable to some other person by his own acts, default or operation of law. The settlement provided that after the determination of the trust in favour of the settlor, the property was to be held on trust with the income to be paid to his wife for life.

HELD: (Ch.) The trust in favour of the wife was valid in the event of an involuntary alienation by operation of law. (1889) 40 Ch. D. 585

COMMENTARY
North J. (at 587–588) stated that " . . . a settlement by a man of his own property upon himself for life, with a clause forfeiting his interest in the event of alienation, or attempted alienation, has never, so far as I know, been defeated in favour of a particular alienee; it has only been defeated in favour of the

settlor's creditors generally, on the ground that it would be a fraud on bankrupt law". Therefore, where the alienation is as a result of some other reason, apart from bankruptcy, the protective trust would be valid.

6. CHARITABLE AND NON CHARITABLE TRUSTS

[A] CHARITABLE TRUSTS

KEY PRINCIPLE: *Charity in its legal sense comprises four principal divisions: trusts for the relief of poverty: trusts for the advancement of education: trusts for the advancement of religion, and trusts for other purposes beneficial to the community.*

The Commissioners for Special Purposes of The Income Tax v. Pemsel 1891

Land was conveyed upon trusts whereby any surplus rents and profits were to be used, amongst other purposes, for the maintenance, support and advancement of missionary establishments abroad of the Moravian Church.

HELD: (HL) The words "charitable" purposes were not restricted to the relief of poverty. [1891] A.C. 531

COMMENTARY
The relative breadth of the formulation and the continued use of analogy to the *Charitable Uses Act 1601* allows for sensible flexibility and responsiveness to modern demands. In *Scottish Burial Reform and Cremation Society Ltd v. Glasgow Corporation* [1968] A.C. 138, the House of Lords held that the premises concerned were used by a charity for charitable purposes and that cremation was for the public benefit within the "spirit and intendment" of the preamble to the 1601 Act. There was sufficient analogy between the present case and references to burial in the preamble and case law relating to burial.

Relief of Poverty

KEY PRINCIPLE: *Poverty does not mean destitution but is a wide term implying deprivation in a relative sense having regard to the circumstances.*

Re Coulthurst 1951

A testator directed that income from the trust fund be applied " . . . for the benefit . . . of the . . . widows and orphaned children of deceased officers and ex-officers of the bank as the bank shall in its absolute discretion consider . . . to be most deserving of such assistance . . . ".

HELD: (CA) The trust was charitable. The intent was that the money go to persons having the quality of poverty within the meaning of the 1601 preamble. [1951] Ch. 661

Re Niyazi's Will Trusts 1978

The testator left the residue of his estate in trust to be used "towards the construction of some working men's hostel" in Famagusta, Cyprus.

HELD: (Ch.) The trust was charitable. The terms "working men's" and "hostel" had sufficient connotation of poverty. [1978] 3 All E.R. 785

COMMENTARY

In *Re Coulthurst* it was said that poverty did not mean destitution; "it is a word of wide and somewhat indefinite import; it may not be unfairly paraphrased for present purposes as meaning persons who have to "go short" in the ordinary acceptance of that term, due regard being had to their status in life". Poverty is therefore a relative concept. Other examples of gifts which have been held to be charitable for the relief of poverty include *Biscoe v. Jackson* (1887) 35 Ch. D. 460 (a gift to establish a soup kitchen in Shoreditch), and *Shaw v. Halifax Corporation* [1915] K.B. 170 (a home for ladies in reduced means).

Public Benefit in the Relief of Poverty

KEY PRINCIPLE: *A gift which is primarily for the relief of poverty, albeit for a particular class of poor people, is for the public benefit and thus charitable.*

Dingle v. Turner 1972

A testator directed that the income of a trust be applied in paying pensions to poor employees of E Ltd, a company jointly owned by the testator.

HELD: (HL) A trust for "poor employees" was capable of being a valid charitable trust. The distinction between charitable trusts and private trusts depended, as a matter of construction, whether the gift was for the relief of poverty amongst a particular description of poor people or was merely a gift to particular poor persons. [1972] A.C. 601

COMMENTARY

In *Re Scarisbrick* [1951] Ch. 622, the Court of Appeal made clear that a different test was to be applied to trusts for the relief of poverty. The House of Lords in the present case followed this view which has since been reiterated in *Re Cohen* [1973] 1 W.L.R. 415 (a gift for relatives "in special" need) and *Re Segelman* [1995] 3 All E.R. 676 (a gift for "poor and needy" members of the family "in order to relieve hardship").

KEY PRINCIPLE: *A scheme can still be of public benefit where beneficiaries might make incidental profits.*

Joseph Rowntree Memorial Trust Housing Association Ltd v. Attorney General 1983

The plaintiff charitable housing trust wished to build dwellings for elderly people The terms of the scheme were that applicants would have to be of a certain age. They would have to pay a capital sum, be able to pay service charges, live independently and be in need of the type of accommodation provided. The Charity Commissioners argued that the scheme was not charitable in that benefits were conferred by contract not bounty.

HELD: (Ch.) In applying the spirit of the 1601 preamble, the beneficiaries could be aged or poor and not necessarily both, though there had to be "relief" of one or other of those conditions. A charitable gift did not have to be made solely by bounty. That the beneficiaries contributed towards the cost of the benefit on a contractual basis and the absence of a termination provision for when a beneficiary ceased to qualify did not prevent the scheme being charitable. The security of tenure was part of the need for accommodation for the elderly which the scheme was relieving. Any profit the beneficiary might make was incidental and not at the expense of the charity; it did not make the scheme as a whole non-charitable. [1983] 2 W.L.R. 284

COMMENTARY
The court took a broad view of the way in which a need can be relieved within the bounds of public benefit. The court's concern was to give effect to the underlying intent of the scheme notwithstanding that to give proper effect to the aim of providing secure housing would stretch the benefit to the individual beyond that which is normally acceptable.

Advancement of education

KEY PRINCIPLE: *Education is to be interpreted broadly to include connected activities.*

Re Mariette 1915
A testator bequeathed money for the purpose of building squash or Eton Fives courts and for the provision of school sports prizes.

HELD: (Ch.) The bequests created valid charitable trusts. Daily sports activities were part of the daily routine of a school. [1915] 2 Ch. 284

COMMENTARY
Gifts to schools and colleges will normally be charitable provided they are used for charitable educational purposes including activities associated with academic education. Similarly, in *Re Dupree's Deed Trusts* [1945] Ch. 16, a gift to promote chess tournaments for schoolboys was held to be charitable. Gifts to educational bodies other than schools may be charitable: *Re Webber* [1954] 1 W.L.R. 1500.

KEY PRINCIPLE: *There must be some element of teaching, instruction or dissemination of knowledge to count as education.*

Re Shaw 1957
George Bernard Shaw bequeathed a fund, the income from which he directed to be used for research into replacing the

present alphabet with another of at least 40 letters, to transliterate one of his plays into the new alphabet and to persuade the government and public to use the new alphabet.

HELD: (Ch.) The trusts were not charitable. An increase in knowledge is not a charitable purpose unless accompanied by teaching or education. Whilst research and propaganda may increase knowledge, any time saved in using the new alphabet was not for the advancement of education. [1957] 1 W.L.R. 729

Re Hopkins 1965
A testator left part of her estate to the Francis Bacon Society, whose aims included the encouragement of the reading of Bacon's work and research to establish whether Shakespeare's works were in fact written by Bacon.

HELD: (Ch.) Research into Shakespeare's scripts was a charitable purpose as any definitive identification of the author would contribute to knowledge. In order for research to count as educational for the purposes of being charitable, it must be of educational value to the researcher or be directed to the dissemination of material so as to improve the sum of communicable knowledge in an area which may be covered by education. [1965] Ch. 669

COMMENTARY
Re Hopkins broadened the courts' approach to education to allow for research provided it involved teaching or instruction or the dissemination of educationally valid material. It would be strange if, for instance medical research organisations were barred from charitable status on the grounds that they were not teaching bodies. Education can be extended to education of artistic taste: *Royal Choral Society v. Commissioners of Inland Revenue* [1943] 2 All E.R. 101.

KEY PRINCIPLE: *There is a threshold of merit in assessing the charitable status of an educational gift.*

Re Pinion 1965
A testator left his studio and its contents including paintings and other *objets d'art* to be endowed as a museum to display his

collection. Experts gave evidence that the collection had no educational merit whatsoever.

HELD: (CA) Where the utility of a gift is in question, the court had to hear expert evidence on the quality and merit of the proposed exhibits in order to judge whether they would be conducive to the education of the public. Although the merit of the collection was a matter of taste, there was an accepted canon of taste. The overwhelming evidence was that the collection was worthless as a means of education and no purpose would be served by foisting on the public a "mass of junk". [1965] Ch. 85

COMMENTARY
The test of merit is fairly minimal but in cases of doubt the court should hear expert evidence. In *Re Delius* [1957] Ch. 299 the merit of Delius' work was clear. Increasing the public's knowledge of Delius's works was held to be charitable within the principles of *Royal Choral Society v. Commissioners of Inland Revenue*, above.

Public Benefit in the Advancement of Education

KEY PRINCIPLE: *The test of public benefit is not satisfied where the beneficiaries are identified on the basis of a personal nexus with the settlor.*

Oppenheim v. Tobacco Securities Trust Co. Ltd 1951
Trustees were directed to apply certain income "in providing for the . . . education of children of employees or former employees" of a British company and its subsidiaries or allied companies. There were 110,000 such employees.

HELD: (HL) Although the group was large, the nexus between them was employment by particular employers. Therefore, the trust did not satisfy the public benefit test to be charitable. [1951] A.C. 297

COMMENTARY
Where there is a personal nexus between the beneficiary and settlor then the test of public benefit is not satisfied. As a matter of public policy, it is difficult to justify tax exemption

for trusts where they are limited by the nature of a person's employment. In *Re Compton* [1945] 1 All E.R. 198 a gift for the education of the descendants of three named people was not charitable as they could not be regarded as a sufficient section of the community.

Advancement of Religion

KEY PRINCIPLE: *Religion for the purpose of charitable status means a theistic belief.*

Bowman v. Secular Society Ltd 1917

The Secular Society was a limited company whose main object was "to promote . . . the principle that human conduct should be based upon natural knowledge and not upon supernatural belief, and that human welfare in this world is the proper end of all thought and action".

HELD: (HL) There was a valid trust in favour of the Society although not a charitable one. [1917] A.C. 406

COMMENTARY
[1] Lord Parker stated that a trust for the purpose of any kind of monotheistic theism would be a valid charitable trust.
[2] The courts do not distinguish between different religions or sects within religions: *Neville Estates v. Madden* [1962] Ch. 832. The courts are willing to accept as charitable peculiar sects, provided that they are not adverse to the foundations of all religion or subversive of morality: *Thornton v. Howe* (1862) 31 Beav. 14 and *Re Watson (Dec'd)* [1973] 1 W.L.R. 1472. Faith healing has been found to be a charitable purpose in *Re Le Cren Clarke* [1996] 1 W.L.R. 288. Ancestor worship has been denied charitable status in *Yeap Cheah Neo v. Ong Cheng Neo* (1875) L.R. 6 P.C. 381.
[3] In *Re South Place Ethical Society* [1980] 1 W.L.R. 1565 the society was held not to have charitable status because, although its objects included the study and dissemination of ethical principles, its beliefs were non-theistic. In *United Grand Lodge of Ancient Free & Accepted Masons of England & Wales v. Holborn Borough Council* [1957] 1 W.L.R. 1080, the freemasons were denied charitable status.

Public Benefit in the Advancement of Religion

KEY PRINCIPLE: *The public benefit of a gift for the purpose of advancement of religion must be susceptible of proof.*

Gilmour v. Coats 1949

Money was to be held on trust for the purposes, if charitable, of a Roman Catholic priory consisting of cloistered nuns who "devoted their lives to prayer, contemplation, penance and self-sanctification". Evidence was given as to Roman Catholic doctrine of the benefit to the public through intercessory prayers and the example of their self-denial.

HELD: (HL) The purposes of the priory were not charitable. The benefits of intercessory prayer were not susceptible to proof and the value of the example of self-denial was too vague. The court needed proof of tangible public benefit. [1949] A.C. 426

COMMENTARY
The House of Lords made the important point that the requirement of public benefit applied equally to the advancement of religion as to other heads of charity. In *Neville Estates v. Madden* [1962] Ch. 832 it was said that the court was entitled to assume that some benefit arose from attendance at a place of worship. In *Re Hetherington* [1989] 2 W.L.R. 1094, the court reverted to a more generous approach. it was held that gifts for the saying of masses, a religious purpose, were prima facie charitable. There was sufficient public benefit so long as the masses were said in public and stipends thereby payable to priests relieved the Church's other funds.

Other Purposes Beneficial to the Community

KEY PRINCIPLE: *Trusts for recreational purposes may be charitable provided they are exclusively charitable or come within the terms of the* Recreational Charities Act 1958.

Inland Revenue Commissioners v. City of Glasgow Police Athletic Association 1953

The association claimed exemption from tax on the profits of their sports event.

HELD: (HL) The association was not exempt as it was not established "for charitable purposes only". Though improving police efficiency through athletic activity could be regarded as charitable, the purpose of providing recreation for members was not exclusively charitable and was not merely incidental to the charitable purposes. [1953] A.C. 380

Inland Revenue Commissioners v. Baddeley 1955

Land was conveyed on trusts to be used for the purpose of the "promotion of the religious, social and physical well-being of persons resident . . . in West Ham and Leyton . . . by the provision of facilities for religious services and instruction and for the social and physical training and recreation of such . . . persons who . . . are in the opinion of such leaders, members or likely to become members of the Methodist Church and of insufficient means otherwise to enjoy the advantages provided by these presents . . . ".

HELD: (HL) The trusts were not charitable. They did not fall within the fourth head of charity of other purposes beneficial to the community. The language of the conveyances was too vague and allowed the property to be used for purposes which were not charitable or if prima facie charitable, was not of sufficient public benefit. The restriction to members or future members of the Methodist Church within a given area constituted a class within a class which did not satisfy the test of public benefit. [1955] A.C. 572

COMMENTARY

[1] In both cases, the purposes in themselves could be charitable, but could only be enjoyed by a limited class of persons. In both cases there was no genuine benefit to a section of the community. As a response to cases such as these, the *Recreational Charities Act 1958* was introduced.

[2] The cases also illustrate the point that some of the requirements for charitable status overlap. The causes here did not satisfy the public benefit test, in that, it was incidental

in *Inland Revenue Commissioners v. City of Glasgow Police Athletic Association* and was limited to an insufficient class in *I.R.C. v. Baddeley*. Moreover, to the extent that the purposes were charitable, they did not satisfy the test of being exclusively charitable as the funds could be used for purposes other than charitable ones.

KEY PRINCIPLE: *Under the Recreational Charities Act 1958, facilities for recreation provided with the object of benefiting a given group could be charitable even where the persons benefiting are not in a position of relative deprivation.*

Guild (Executor Nominate of the late James Young Russell) v. Inland Revenue Commissioners 1992

A testator left the residue of his estate: "to the town council of North Berwick for the use in connection with the Sports Centre in North Berwick or some similar purpose in connection with sport". The I.R.C. argued that this bequest was not charitable and thus not tax exempt.

HELD: (HL) On the true construction of section 1 (2)(a) of the *Recreational Charities Act 1958*, facilities for recreation or other leisure time occupation could be provided for improving the conditions of the persons for whom they were primarily intended notwithstanding that those persons were not in a position of relative social disadvantage or suffering a degree of deprivation. The facilities concerned were provided in the interests of social welfare within the meaning of section 1 of the Act. [1992] 2 W.L.R. 397

COMMENTARY

The Act provides that facilities for recreation are deemed to be charitable if they are in the social interest and for the public benefit. This would be the case if they were provided to a group in need such as the young or infirm or if the facilities were available to the public at large.

KEY PRINCIPLE: *The purposes which are beneficial to the community and regarded as charitable are not a closed or predefined group.*

Incorporated Council of Law Reporting for England and Wales v. Attorney-General 1972

The primary purpose of the Incorporated Society was: "The preparation and publication . . . at a modest price and under gratuitous professional control, of reports of judicial decisions of the superior and appellate courts in England."

HELD: (CA) The Society was an educational charity. It was also said that it could be regarded as coming under the fourth head of purposes beneficial to the community. [1972] Ch. 73

COMMENTARY
[1] Other objects which have been held to be charitable under the fourth head include: gifts for a voluntary fire brigade (*Re Wokingham Fire Brigade Trusts* [1951] Ch. 373) and gifts for the preservation of places of historical importance or beauty (*Re Cranstoun's Will Trusts* [1949] 1 Ch. 523).
[2] An organisation to promote a profession and benefit its members is not charitable (*General Nursing Council for England and Wales v. St Marylebone Borough Council*) [1959] A.C. 540
[3] In *Re Foveaux* [1895] W.N. 29, the anti-vivisection society was held to be charitable but this was successfully challenged in *National Anti-Vivisection Society v. Inland Revenue Commissioners* [1948] A.C. 31. In the latter case, it was found that the alleviation of animal suffering was outweighed by the public benefit of vivisection in advancing medical research.
[4] Animal charities are usually accepted as being of public benefit as enhancing humane behaviour as in *Re Wedgwood* [1915] 1 Ch. 113 and *Re Moss* [1949] 1 All E.R. 495. Animal homes and hospitals are normally accepted as being charitable as in *Re Douglas* (1887) 35 Ch. D. 472, though, in *Re Grove-Grady* [1929] 1 Ch. 557, an animal sanctuary failed as the animals were to be left alone without public access.

KEY PRINCIPLE: *Political trusts aiming to change the law are not charitable.*

McGovern v. Attorney–General 1982

Amnesty International was founded with the object of securing the observance of the human rights of prisoners of conscience throughout the world. It sought charitable status for part of its activity including the relief of prisoners of conscience and their families, securing the release of prisoners, campaigning for the abolition of torture and other inhuman treatment and promoting research into the observance of human rights. It set up a trust deed to cover these objects for which it claimed charitable status.

HELD: (Ch.) Though the relief of human suffering was charitable in its nature, it would not be charitable if any of its main objects were political. Trusts seeking to change the law of the U.K. or another country or seeking to alter government policy or administrative decisions were of a political nature. The object of securing the release of political prisoners through lawful persuasion to change the law, policy or administration of a country was political. That object affected all the other objects in the deed thus making it non-charitable. In particular, the object of procuring abolition of torture and inhuman treatment was a political purpose as it sought to change legislation. Further, the objects of researching into human rights would add to the sum of knowledge and be of public benefit but in the context they were merely adjunct to the other political purposes. [1982] Ch. 321

COMMENTARY

[1] Historically, the courts have been wary of trusts which use the accepted heads of charity as a guise for advancing political aims which of themselves are not charitable. In *Re Hopkinson* [1949] W.N. 29, a trust to advance education in accordance with the Labour Party manifesto was held not to be charitable. In *Re Strakosch* [1949] Ch. 529, it was held that a trust to strenghten unity in South Africa through improving relations between the English and Dutch communities was not charitable as it had a political character. Where a trust may appear to be political, but argues that it is for the public benefit, the court is placed in an iniquitous position of appearing to determine the public benefit of the cause espoused.

[2] In *Re Koeppler's Will Trusts* [1984] 2 W.L.R. 973, a gift was made to the Wilton Park Centre which was a prestigious body which organized conferences on international political

affairs with representatives from institutions such as NATO, OECD and the EEC. The Court of Appeal found that the trust was valid as advancing education and that any political content was incidental as the centre had no political affiliation.

Exclusively Charitable

KEY PRINCIPLE: *A gift must be devoted to solely charitable purposes to acquire charitable status.*

Chichester Diocesan Fund and Board of Finance v. Simpson 1944

A testator left the residue of his estate to be applied "for such charitable institution or institutions or other charitable or benevolent object or objects in England".

HELD: (HL) The bequest was void for uncertainty. The word "benevolent" had a wider meaning than charitable. The word "or" permitted a choice between "charitable" and "benevolent". Thus, non-charitable benevolent purposes could be selected, meaning that the bequest was not exclusively charitable. In the absence of exclusive charitable intent, the gift also failed as a trust because there was no certainty of beneficiaries. [1944] A.C. 341

COMMENTARY
[1] Similarly, in *Blair v. Duncan* [1902] A.C. 37, a bequest "for such charitable or public purposes as my trustee thinks proper" failed because some or all of the funds could have been used for "public purposes which were not charitable". The Privy Council in *Att.-Gen. of the Bahamas v. Royal Trust Co* [1986] 3 All E.R. 323 also read the bequest disjunctively. One might think that the courts might take a more "charitable" reading of such bequests, but, in the absence of certain words and evidence, the court cannot second guess a testator's intent. *The Charitable Trusts (Validation) Act 1954* does save such ambiguous bequests but only for dispositions made before 1953.
[2] Where non-charitable purposes are wholly subsidiary to the charity, the gift may be valid. In *London Hospital Medical College v. Inland Revenue Commissioners* [1976] 1 W.L.R. 613, it was held that a Students' Union was charitable although it provided specific benefits to its members because

these were incidental to its overall charitable educational purpose.

The *cy-près* Doctrine

KEY PRINCIPLE: *A charitable fund may be applied cy-pres to give effect to the spirit of the gift.*

Peggs v. Lamb 1994

Ancient rights of grazing on certain areas of land existed in favour of the freemen of Huntingdon. By 1829, these included the right to income from other uses of the land. Later, the land became vested in Huntingdon Corporation upon trust for the freeman. Parts of the land were sold; the capital was placed in a separate fund the income of which also being held on trust for the freemen. By 1960, the trusts were recognised as charities for the provision of income for the freeman and their widows. By 1991, there were only 34 possible beneficiaries yet the annual income was £550,000 and the assets were £4 m in cash and 700 acres of agricultural land. The trustees believed that annual distribution amongst the class was no longer consistent with a charitable application. They proposed an application to only freemen and their widows in need with the surplus applied to the sick and needy of the borough.

HELD: (Ch.) The provision of funds to a class was not of itself charitable and had to be interpreted within the preamble to the *Charitable Uses Act 1601*. The size of the fund and decline in number of freeman had led to an equal distribution falling outside that spirit. Having regard to the spirit of the gift the freemen had now ceased to be a suitable class by reference to which the charitable purpose could be carried out. Consequently, a *cy-près* scheme under section 13 of the *Charities Act 1913* would be settled so as to extend the class to all the inhabitants of the borough. [1994] Ch. 172

COMMENTARY
Section 13 of the 1960 Act (now the 1993 Act) serve to extend the jurisdiction to apply a *cy-près* scheme beyond instances of impossibility or impracticality to now allow for the spirit of bequests to be given effect.

KEY PRINCIPLE: *Where a gift fails from the outset, the court will not direct a cy-près application unless they are satisfied that the testator had a general charitable intention.*

Re Rymer 1895

A testator bequeathed £5,000 to the rector for the time being of St Thomas' Seminary for the education of priests in the diocese of Westminister for the purposes of such seminary. The seminary closed just before the testator's death.

HELD: (CA) The bequest was for the particular institution. The institution having ceased to exist during the testator's lifetime, the legacy could not be applied *cy-près* and fell into the residue. [1895] 1 Ch. 19

COMMENTARY

[1] It was clear from the evidence that the testator's gift was specific and did not evince a general charitable intention. In *Biscoe v. Jackson* [1887] 35 Ch. D. 460, money was left to establish a soup kitchen in Shoreditch. The intended land was not available upon the testator's death but it was held that the money could be re-applied as the general charitable intention existed to benefit the poor and sick of the area.

[2] Where a gift is to a corporate charity, there has been a tendency to assume that the gift is for that specific body and that where the gift is to an unincorporated charity the assumption is usually that the gift is to the purpose of that charity and is more easily re-applied to another charity with the same purpose. See *Re Vernon's Will Trusts* [1972] Ch. 300 and Re *Finger's Will Trusts* [1972] Ch. 286. In *Re Spence* [1979] Ch. 283, this line was followed where a gift to a specific old folks' home was held to be for that institution and not for the general purpose of providing for the elderly. In the absence of a general charitable intention, no *cy-près* scheme could be applied. A gift to a specific institution can be applied to successor bodies or amalgamated bodies even if the purposes are slightly wider though not if they are significantly different: *Re Faraker* [1912] 2 Ch. 488.

[3] There is said to be initial failure of a gift when it cannot take effect upon the death of the testator. Where the gift can take effect but later fails because the object ceases to exist, then that is called subsequent failure. Where there is subsequent failure, there is no need to establish general charitable intention

in order to make a *cy-près* application because the gift did take effect as a charitable gift, albeit failing subsequently.

[B] NON CHARITABLE TRUSTS

KEY PRINCIPLE: *A private trust must have a beneficiary capable of enforcing the trust.*

Re Astor 1952

A settlement contained trusts which included the "maintenance of . . . good understanding . . . between nations, . . . the preservation of the independence and integrity of newspapers . . . and the protection of newspapers . . . from being absorbed or controlled by combines". It was agreed that the purposes were not charitable but were within the rule against perpetuities.

HELD: (Ch.) The trusts were invalid because they were not for the benefit of individuals but for non-charitable purposes which no-one could enforce. The purposes were also void for uncertainty. [1952] Ch. 534

COMMENTARY
Where a gift is intended to be for a charitable purpose but which is held to be not charitable then the gift to the non-charitable purpose will not take effect as a trust, as in *Re Shaw*, above. Where the trust is invalid then the property will go to the giftover, if any, or on resulting trust or ultimately become *bona vacantia* if there is no other potential recipient.

KEY PRINCIPLE: *There are exceptions to the rule requiring beneficiaries.*

Re Hooper 1932

A testator bequeathed money out of which income was to be applied "so far as they legally can do so and in any manner that they may in their discretion arrange" for the care and upkeep of certain graves, a vault, certain monuments, a tablet and a window.

HELD: (Ch.) The money was not given to the trustees beneficially but was held on trust for the horses and hounds so long as they shall live. (1889) 41 Ch. D. 552

COMMENTARY

[1] The rule against perpetuities did not apply to the church tablet and window. The court kept the other parts of the bequest within the rule by restricting the validity of the gift to 21 years. The result in allowing for a non-charitable purpose trust still leaves the question as to who could enforce the trust. It may have been better to attribute by analogy charitable status to the purposes. In *Re Dean*, the time limit was thought to satisfy the rule against perpetuity.

[2] In addition to trusts for the erection and maintenance of monuments and graves, and maintenance of animals, other types of purpose trusts which have been recognized include:

(a) trusts for saying of masses (*Bourne v. Keane* [1919] A.C. 815) though these can now be regarded as charitable anyway as in *Re Hetherington*, above.

(b) possibly, trusts for unincorporated associations, see *Re Lipinsky's Will Trust* below.

(c) and other miscellaneous trusts (*Re Thompson* [1934] Ch. 342, a bequest to be applied for the promotion and furtherance of fox-hunting).

KEY PRINCIPLE: *The court will not extend the class of anomalous purpose trusts unless they have a sufficiently certain purpose.*

Re Endacott 1960

(See Chap. 4).

HELD: (CA) The bequest did not fall within the anomalous class of non-charitable purpose trusts as it was too wide and uncertain in nature to be enforceable. [1960] Ch. 232

COMMENTARY

For a non-charitable purpose trust to be accepted it must fall clearly within the recognised classes of purpose trusts otherwise it will not be valid.

KEY PRINCIPLE: *A gift for an unincorporated association may be valid if, though, described for a purpose, there is a benefit for ascertained or ascertainable beneficiaries.*

Re Denley's Trust Deed 1969

Trusts were declared of land to be used for recreation, primarily as a sports ground for employees of the company and such other persons as the trustees may allow. If less than 75 per cent of employees subscribed to use the sport ground, the land was to be conveyed to a hospital. The trustees sought a determination as to whether there was a valid trust or whether the gift-over to the hospital should take effect.

HELD: (Ch.) The trust was valid because, though the trust was not charitable and though expressed for purposes rather than beneficiaries, the purpose was directly or indirectly for the benefit of individuals. The class of employees was sufficiently ascertainable and the class of other persons was a valid power from which every member need not be identified. The court could enforce the trust by restraining improper use of the land or by ordering the trustee to allow employees and others to use the land for recreation. [1969] 1 Ch. 373

Re Lipinsky's Will Trusts 1976

A testator left part of his estate to the Hull Judeans (Maccabi) Association to be used solely in constructing and improving the new buildings for the association. At the time of his death, the association was not charitable. It did not have premises of its own at that time but did acquire its own premises subsequently. Another part was left to the Hull Hebrew Board of Deputies, which was charitable, for the sole purpose of constructing and improving the new buildings for the "association". The executors sought a determination as to whether the bequests were valid or void for impracticality.

HELD: (Ch.) The gift (though to a non-charitable unincorporated association) was valid as there were ascertainable beneficiaries, *i.e.* the members of the association and the purpose of the bequest was within the powers of the association. Notwithstanding the word "solely", they could vary the trust. The term "new buildings" meant whatever buildings the association had or chose to build or buy; the reference to improvements did not mean such continuity so as break the rule against perpetuities. The rules of the association were sufficient to regulate the purpose in the bequest. [1976] Ch. 235

COMMENTARY

[1] The modern approach to purpose trusts of non-charitable unincorporated associations is that they are valid if there are individuals who benefit, a clear purpose and some way of regulating the bequest within the intended purpose. The regulation may in fact be self-regulation. The courts may well take into account the character of the recipients such as in *Leahy v. Att.-Gen. of New South Wales* [1959] A.C. 457 where the trust was in favour of an order of contemplative nuns.

[2] Earlier cases had considered a variety of possible interpretations of gifts to non-charitable unincorporated associations. *Re Recher's Will Trusts* [1972] Ch. 526 and *Neville Estates v. Madden* [1962] Ch. 832, indicate four possibilities:

(a) a gift to the current members to be distributed amongst themselves;

(b) a gift to present and future members (though such a gift would have to be phrased to come within the rule against perpetuities);

(c) a gift to the officers of the association to be held on trust to carry out the purposes of the trust;

(d) a gift to the existing members to be managed according to the rules of the association but not divisible amongst existing members; each member's "share" accruing to future members.

In *Re Recher's Will Trusts* an absolute gift to an anti-vivisection society was held to be a gift to the members of that society (not those of the larger society into which it later amalgamated). The gift was not to the individual members to distribute amongst themselves but was to be treated as an accretion to the funds which constituted the subject matter of the contract between the members. However, since the society had dissolved before the will was made, the gift failed. The fourth interpretation, which was applied in the case, is reconcilable with the approach in *Denley* and *Lipinsky*, though, in the latter case, the court seems to have allowed more leeway to the members in applying the purpose than was intended in the bequest.

[3] Gifts to associations which are not unincorporated (there being no possibility of a trust or a *Recher* type solution) have been treated on an agency or mandate basis, *i.e.* the gift is

deemed to be given for a given purpose, which if not satisfied is returnable on the ground that the agency or mandate has not been performed. See *Conservative and Unionist Central Office v. Burrell* [1982] 1 W.L.R. 522.

7. RESULTING TRUSTS

Introduction

A resulting trust is one type of implied trust, the constructive trust being the other. Implied trusts are not expressly created but take effect by operation of law. A conventional classification of resulting trusts includes the automatic and presumed resulting trusts.

Automatic Resulting Trusts

KEY PRINCIPLE: *An automatic resulting trust arises where the purpose of a trust fails.*

Barclays Bank Ltd v. Quistclose Investments Ltd 1970

R Ltd decided to declare dividends on its share but was unable to pay for it. The defendant provided R Ltd with a loan for the purpose of paying for this dividend. The money was deposited in a separate account with the plaintiff. The plaintiff agreed that the money was to be used for the payment of the dividend. R Ltd went into liquidation with substantial debts before the dividend was paid. The defendant claimed to be entitled to the money in the separate account.

HELD: (HL) The arrangement for payment of creditors (the shareholders) by the defendant constituted a trust for the shareholders, which if it failed, would lead to a resulting trust for the defendant. That the transaction was a loan did not prevent it from simultaneously being a trust. As the money was not used for its intended purpose, there was a remedy in equity of a resulting trust as there was evidence that it was intended that if the primary use of the money was not fulfilled that the money should return to the lender. The plaintiff having received the money with knowledge of its intended use, could not withhold the money from the defendant but held it as constructive trustees. [1970] A.C. 567

Carreras Rothmans Ltd v. Freeman Mathews Treasure Ltd 1984

The plaintiff paid a monthly sum to its advertising agent to pay invoices incurred in placing the plaintiff's adverts. Because of the defendant's financial difficulties, an agreement was made whereby money was put into a separate account specifically for the purpose of paying the previous month's invoices. The defendant went into liquidation.

HELD: (Ch.) The money in the separate account was transferred for a purpose which had not been fulfilled. As there had been a clear agreement, the money should revert back to the plaintiff. The money was never the defendant's beneficially; there was an incomplete transfer leading to the money reverting to the settlor. [1984] 3 W.L.R. 1016

COMMENTARY

[1] In *Westdeutsche Landesbank Girozentrale v. Islington Borough Council* [1996] A.C. 669, it was held that the council must return with compound interest, money received under an *ultra vires* interest swap agreement. One of the reasons was that there was a resulting trust of the money back to the bank in the light of the incomplete transfer to the council given its *ultra vires* nature.

[2] *Quistclose* also illustrates the need to distinguish the basis for implied trusts. There was an automatic resulting trust because the purpose having not been completed there was an incomplete transfer. The bank also held the property on trust for them, but as a constructive trustee based upon them having had notice of the agreement.

[3] Other instances of where a resulting trust automatically arises include:

(a) Where an express trust fails: *Re Ames' Settlement* [1946] Ch. 217.

(b) Where an attempted charitable trust fails: *Chichester Diocesan Fund and Board of Finance v. Simpson* [1944] A.C. 341.

(c) Where the settlor has failed to dispose of the entire beneficial interest in a property. This can arise where a trust is created for a beneficiary for life but there is no giftover once that beneficiary dies; at that point there is a resulting trust to the settlor. See *Vandervell v. I.R.C.* (see Chap. 4).

(d) Where the beneficial interest is not wholly exhausted. This can take place where money is advanced to an unincorporated association which subsequently ceases to exist. The money could revert to the settlor on resulting trust (see below). A similar situation can arise where money is donated for a purpose which is no longer necessary. In *Re Gillingham Bus Disaster fund* [1958] Ch. 300, funds were raised following a disaster in which twenty four marine cadets were killed. Later, the funds were proved unnecessary. The court held that the funds should revert to the donors on a resulting trust and that money from unidentified donors should be paid into court rather than to the Crown. It was clear that their contributions were meant for the disaster victims and not for the Crown.

KEY PRINCIPLE: *Upon the dissolution of an incorporated association any surplus funds should be distributed to its surviving members according to their contractual rights.*

Re Bucks Constabulary Widows' and Orphans' Fund Friendly Society (No. 2) 1979

The Society was open to serving members of the Bucks constabulary. In 1968 the constabulary was amalgamated with others. The members resolved to wind up the society, continue to pay benefits to its existing beneficiaries until dissolution and realise its assets for the purchase of annuities for all current members and the transfer of some of its assets to the Thames Valley Constabulary Benevolent Fund. The instrument of dissolution provided for the purchase of the annuities and the transfer of £40,000 to the Thames Valley Fund with the surplus going to another benevolent fund. The trustee sought a determination as to whether the society's funds could be distributed according to the terms of the instrument of dissolution.

HELD: (Ch.) There was a general principle applicable to all unincorporated societies under a contract between a society and its members, that any surplus funds remaining upon a society's dissolution should belong to the existing members.

Subject to contrary expression such a term should be implied. The entitlement of the members were governed by the contract between them. The instrument of dissolution signed by some members did not constitute directions by all members as to how their interest in the surplus funds should be distributed. [1979] 1 W.L.R. 936

COMMENTARY

[1] Where an unincorporated association ends, the remaining funds should be distributed to existing beneficiaries according to the contract between the association and the members. When there are no beneficiaries left, any surplus may go to the Crown as *bona vacantia.* However, before that stage is reached, it is not open to the association to give funds, which should be held on trust for the members, to third parties. In *Re GKN Bolts and Nuts (Automotive Division) Birmingham Works, Sports and Social Club* [1982] 1 W.L.R. 774, it was held that where surplus funds are to be distributed to surviving members, this should be done, subject to contrary contractual expression, on an equal basis irrespective of the duration of membership or value of contributions.

[2] There are three main approaches as to how funds from a dissolved unincorporated association should be distributed:

(a) The property should be distributed upon resulting trust to those who contributed the property: *Re Printers and Transferrers Amalgamated Trades Protection Society* [1899] 2 A.C. 386. This approach is no longer used in the situation of unincorporated associations, though it prevails in situations of imperfect dispositions.

(b) The property should be distributed on a contractual basis. Prior to *Re Bucks Constabulary Widows' and Orphans' Fund Friendly Society,* it was held in *Re St Andrews Allotment Association* [1969] 1 W.L.R. 229 that the contributions of donors including members ceased to be their property once the contribution was made and were not held on trust for those contributors. The contributions were complete and became the property of the association and should be distributed upon dissolution in accordance with the association's rules to the members. In *Re Sick and Funeral Society of St John's Sunday School* [1973] Ch. 51, the same approach was taken. It was also said that the distribution should be on a per capita basis.

(c) The property should go as bona vacantia to the crown. In *Re West Sussex Constabulary Widows, Children and Benevolent (1930) Fund Trusts* [1970] Ch. 1, the association was wound up. The court held that identified legacies should revert to the donors on resulting trust and unidentified donations should go to the Crown as *bona vacantia*. Here the members were not beneficiaries so distribution amongst surviving members was not appropriate.

In *Davis v. Richards & Wallington Industries Ltd* [1990] 1 W.L.R. 1511 the winding up of a pension scheme was considered. It was said *obiter* that employer's contributions could go on resulting trust where the contributions were for a limited purpose and that the surplus of employees' contributions could go as *bona vacantia* as the employees were limited by statute as to the benefit they could receive.

Presumed Resulting Trusts

KEY PRINCIPLE: *A resulting trust may arise from a voluntary conveyance where there is no intention to make a gift.*

Hodgson v. Marks 1971
In 1960, the plaintiff executed a voluntary conveyance in favour of E, her lodger. E was registered as the new proprietor though there was an oral agreement that the plaintiff retained beneficial ownership. The plaintiff and lodger continued to live in the house. In 1964, E sold the property to the first defendant who mortgaged it to the second defendant. The first defendant was registered as the new owner subject to the second defendant's charge. When the plaintiff discovered the situation, she applied for a declaration that the first defendant should transfer the property to her free of the charge against it.

HELD: (CA) On the evidence, the transfer to E was not intended to be a gift. A resulting trust of the beneficial interest arose. In addition, the plaintiff was in actual occupation for the purposes of section 70(1)(g) of the *Land Registration Act 1925* and so had an overriding interest against the defendants. [1971] Ch. 892

COMMENTARY

[1] This is notwithstanding section 60(3) of the *Law of Property Act 1925* which provides that in a voluntary conveyance, a resulting trust shall not be implied merely by reason that the property is not expressed to be conveyed for the use or benefit of the grantee. On the other hand, the failure to satisfy the requirements for creating an express trust in section 53(1) of the *Law of Property Act 1925* did not preclude the existence of a resulting trust based on the intention of the parties.

[2] Other instances where presumed resulting trusts arise include:

(a) Where a purchaser buys a property and puts it in the name of a another person who provides no consideration a resulting trust is presumed in favour of the purchaser: *Dyer v. Dyer* (1788) 2 Cox. E.Q. 92.

(b) Where a purchaser buys a property and puts it in the names of himself and another person who provides no consideration, a resulting trust is presumed whereby the purchaser and other person hold the property on trust for the purchaser. The same applies where the owner of property transfers property into joint names: *Re Vinogradoff* [1935] W.N. 68.

(c) Where two purchasers buy a property together but transfer the title to one of their names only, a resulting trust will be presumed whereby the title owner holds the property on trust for both purchasers: *Bull v. Bull* [1955] 1 Q.B. 234.

KEY PRINCIPLE: *A presumption of a resulting trust may be rebutted by evidence of intention*

Fowkes v. Pascoe 1875

A testator bought shares in the name of herself and the defendant, the son of her daughter-in-law. By her will, she left the residue of her estate to her daughter-in-law for life and thereafter to the defendant and his sister. The question arose as to whether the shares bought in the name of the defendant and the testator were gifted to the defendant or held by him on resulting trust for the testator.

HELD: (CA) On the evidence, the shares had been gifted to the defendant. The testator was wealthy and was fond of the defendant. At the same time as the purchase of the shares, she purchased other shares in the name of herself and her companion. If she had intended all the shares to be held beneficially for herself, there would have been no point in the separate but contemporaneous transactions. (1875) L.R. 10 Ch. App. 343

COMMENTARY
There are frequently evidential problems in providing proof of intention which would rebut the presumption of a resulting trust. See *Sekhon v. Alissa* [1989] 2 F.L.R. 94.

KEY PRINCIPLE: *A presumption of a resulting trust may be rebutted by the presumption of advancement.*

Re Roberts 1964
An insurance policy was taken out by a father on his son. The father paid the premiums and it was argued that on the father's death that the premiums paid were recoverable by his estate.

HELD: (Ch.) The presumption of advancement was applicable. Each payment of the premium was to be regarded as a separate advancement during the father's lifetime. However, the premiums which were paid after the father's death would be recoverable as the relationship had ended by his death. [1964] Ch. 1

COMMENTARY
[1] The presumption of advancement means that in certain situations where one party transfers property to another there is a legal presumption that the transfer was intended as a gift. The presumption can be rebutted by evidence that a gift was not intended, in which case, the presumption of a resulting trust is restored. A transaction such of this could also be interpreted as a loan.
[2] Instances in which the presumption of advancement arises include:

(a) A transfer from father to his legitimate children (*Re Roberts*, above), or a transfer from a person standing *in loco parentis* to the children (*Shephard v. Cartwright* [1955] A.C. 431).
(b) A transfer from a husband to his wife: *Re Eykyn's Trusts* (1877) 6 Ch.D. 115.

[3] Instances in which the presumption of advancement does not arise include:

(a) A transfer from a wife to her husband: *Mercier v. Mercier* (1903) 2 Ch.D. 98.
(b) A transfer from mother to her children: *Bennet v. Bennet* (1879) 10 Ch.D. 474.

KEY PRINCIPLE: *The presumption of advancement can itself be rebutted by evidence.*

Re Gooch 1890

A father bought shares in his son's name in order to allow him to be a director of a company. The son passed all the dividends back to the father and allowed the father keep the share certificate.

HELD: On the evidence, the presumption of advancement was rebutted. (1890) L.T. 383

COMMENTARY

This presumption of advancement is historically based in a time when it was assumed that a man would provide for his wife and children. In today's more equal and complex family situations, the presumption may be weaker. In *McGrath v. Wallis*, *The Times*, April 13, 1995, the Court of Appeal suggested that the presumption was a judicial instrument of last resort.

KEY PRINCIPLE: *A transferor may not rely on an illegal transaction to support a claim to a property by a presumption of a resulting trust or rebuttal of a presumption of advancement.*

Tinsley v. Milligan 1994

The parties bought a house in the plaintiff's name on the understanding that they were joint beneficial owners. This was for the purpose of perpetrating various frauds which continued over a period of time. The defendant later admitted the frauds. The plaintiff moved out of the house and claimed possession. She sought a declaration that she was the sole owner. The defendant counterclaimed for an order of sale of the house and a declaration that the house was held on trust by the plaintiff for both of them in equal shares. In the Court of Appeal, the plaintiff's appeal was dismissed on the ground that public conscience would not be affronted by allowing the defendant's claim on the property.

HELD: (HL) A claimant to an interest in a property was entitled to succeed if the claim did not rely on pleading an illegality notwithstanding that the title was acquired in the course of an illegal transaction. The defendant's contribution to the purchase price, along with the understanding of joint beneficial interest, was sufficient to establish a resulting trust in her favour. The public conscience test was not appropriate in determining to what extent illegal transactions should be recognised. [1994] 1 A.C. 340

Tribe v. Tribe 1995

The plaintiff owned 459 out of 500 shares in the family company. The landlords of two premises served schedules of dilapidations on him which required substantial repairs. As he was the tenant of the premises, he was given legal advice that if the claims were valid he might have to sell the company or dispose of his shares. The plaintiff transferred his shares to the defendant, who was one of his sons. The transfer was expressed to be for consideration of £78,030 but this was never paid nor intended to be paid. In the end, the repairs were not needed. The plaintiff sought the retransfer of the shares but the defendant refused. The plaintiff brought an action claiming that the defendant held the shares as bare trustee and that he had agreed to redeliver them upon demand or at such time as the dispute as to repairs was resolved.

HELD: (CA) A transferor who transferred property for illegal purposes was entitled to withdraw from the transaction before the illegal purpose was carried out and cite the illegal purpose as evidence to rebut the presumption of advancement. This would be an exception to the principle that a court will not aid a person who relies on an illegal act. The plaintiff had in fact not defrauded the creditors. The evidence clearly rebutted the presumption of advancement. [1995] 4 All E.R. 236

COMMENTARY

[1] The underlying rule is that a claimant cannot rely on the evidence an illegal act in order to sustain a claim to a beneficial interest in property either in support of the presumption of a resulting trust or in rebuttal of the presumption of advancement. In *Tinsley v. Milligan*, the defendant was able to sustain the presumption of a resulting trust because she was not relying on an illegal act to support her claim having already acquired a beneficial interest in the property, notwithstanding that the property was intended to be used for an illegal purpose. In *Tribe v. Tribe*, the plaintiff was able to rebut the presumption of advancement because the evidence used to support it, though illegal in intent was never carried out.

[2] More straightforward cases include *Tinker v. Tinker* [1970] P. 136, where it was held that a husband transferred property to his wife in order to defeat his creditors, the presumption of advancement applied and the unlawful purpose could not be used to rebut the presumption. In *Heseltine v. Heseltine* [1971] 1 W.L.R. 342, a wife transferred property to her husband to enable him to qualify as a "name" at Lloyds. Notwithstanding that this purpose was a deception, the court held that the husband should hold the property on resulting trust for the wife. That the marriage had now ended perhaps influenced the court in allowing the wife to, in effect, cite an illegal purpose in support of her claim to a resulting trust.

8. CONSTRUCTIVE TRUSTS

Introduction

A constructive trust arises generally by operation of law rather than by the intention of the parties.

Profits from a Trust

KEY PRINCIPLE: *Where a trustee or fiduciary makes a profit from the trust, a constructive trust will be imposed.*

Keech v. Sandford 1726
(See Chap. 10).

HELD: (Ch.) The trustee held the renewed lease on trust for the infant beneficiary. (1726) Sel. Cas. Ch. 61

COMMENTARY
The trust in that case was a constructive trust for the infant beneficiary. In *Boardman v. Phipps* [1967] 2 A.C. 46, (see Chap. 10) the majority of their Lordships held that a constructive trust was imposed. However, the House of Lords did not appear to distinguish between the duty to account and the imposition of a constructive trust. The distinction is important in cases where the profit has been invested successfully resulting in further profits or where the trustee or fiduciary is adjudicated a bankrupt. In these situations, the constructive trustee can claim the profit or priority over the unsecured creditors.

Receipt of Bribes

KEY PRINCIPLE: *Where a bribe has been received by a fiduciary to betray his fiduciary obligations, the fiduciary is accountable under a constructive trust.*

Attorney-General for Hong Kong v. Reid 1994
The defendant who was a public prosecutor in Hong Kong, breached his fiduciary duty to the Crown and was convicted of corruption. He was, *inter alia*, ordered to pay HK$12.4m to the Crown. Caveats were lodged on titles to property in New Zealand which were in the defendant's and his nominees' name. An application was made by the Att.-Gen. to renew the caveats on the basis that the title to these properties were held on a constructive trust for the Crown.

HELD: (PC) Where a fiduciary accepted a bribe to betray his fiduciary obligations, the bribe and the property representing the bribe including any profit resulting from the use of the money, is held on a constructive trust for the person to whom the duty is owed. The New Zealand properties were therefore held on trust for the Crown to extent that they represented the bribes. The caveats would therefore be renewed. [1994] 1 A.C. 324

COMMENTARY

In *Lister & Co. v. Stubbs* (1890) 45 Ch. D. 1, it was decided that where bribes were received, the liability of the fiduciary was personal, giving rise to a relationship of creditor and debtor only rather than that of trustee and beneficiary. In *Attorney-General for Hong Kong v. Reid, Lister & Co v. Stubbs* was disapproved of. Although the disapproval of the decision in *Lister & Co. v. Stubbs* is clear and correct on equitable principles, but it has been suggested in *Att.-Gen. v. Blake* [1996] 3 W.L.R. 741 that *Lister & Co v. Stubbs* is still binding on the High Court.

Liability of Strangers to the Trust

KEY PRINCIPLE: *Strangers to the trust can be liable as constructive trustees.*

Barnes v. Addy 1874

A, the surviving trustee of a trust fund, where one part was settled upon A's wife and his children and the other part upon B's wife and children, appointed B as sole trustee of half of the fund. B misappropriated that half of the fund and was adjudicated a bankrupt. A's solicitor had advised A against the appointment of B as sole trustee of half the fund but nonetheless prepared the deeds of appointment and an indemnity for B's execution. B appointed another solicitor who warned B's wife of the risk of the transaction but B's wife confirmed that she had no objections to it. The issue was whether the solicitors were liable to make good the loss to the trust.

HELD: (HL) As neither of the solicitors had any knowledge of, or reason to suspect, any dishonest design in the transaction and as the funds had not passed into their hands, the action against them would be dismissed.(1874) L.R. 9 Ch. 244

COMMENTARY

The dictum of Lord Selborne L.C. is important. His Lordship stated (at 251–252) that ". . . strangers are not to be made constructive trustees merely because they act as the agents of trustees in transactions within their legal powers . . . unless those agents receive and become chargeable with some part of the trust property, or unless they assist with knowledge in a dishonest and fraudulent design on the part of the trustees". The liabilities of strangers were categorised until recently as "knowing assistance" and "knowing receipt". However, as a result of the Privy Council decision in *Royal Brunei Airlines Sdn. Bhd. v. Tan* [1995] 2 A.C. 378, the first category is now called dishonest assistance. It has been suggested that it would also be inappropriate to call the second category knowing receipt but rather as "liability for receipt".

KEY PRINCIPLE: *A stranger is liable as a constructive trustee where there has been dishonest assistance in the trustee's breach of trust.*

Royal Brunei Airlines Sdn. Bhd. v. Tan 1995

The plaintiff appointed Borneo Leisure Travel (BLT) as its agent for the sale of passenger and cargo transportation. The defendant was the principal shareholder and managing director of the company. It was agreed that BLT was to hold in trust for the plaintiff money received from its sales of tickets until it was accounted to the plaintiff. However, BLT, with the knowledge and assistance of the defendant, paid the money into its current account instead of a separate account. BLT subsequently became insolvent and the plaintiff commenced an action against the defendant to recover monies due to it.

HELD: (PC) A stranger who dishonestly assisted a trustee to commit a breach of trust or procured him to do so would be liable as a constructive trustee for the loss to the beneficiary. The stranger must however, have acted dishonestly and not merely negligently. It did not matter that the trustee may not have been dishonest or fraudulent nor had received trust property. The defendant was liable to the plaintiff for the whole amount owed by BLT because he had allowed BLT to commit a breach of trust by using the money which it was to hold on trust for the plaintiff when he knew that BLT did not have the authority or power to do so. [1995] 2 A.C. 378

COMMENTARY

[1] The Privy Council was of the view that the term "dishonest assistance" was to be used rather than "knowing assistance", as the phrase knowingly was open to different interpretations. Lord Nicholls (p. 392) stated that "dishonesty is a necessary ingredient of accessory liability. It is also a sufficient ingredient. A liability in equity . . . attaches to a person who dishonestly procures or assists in a breach of trust . . . It is not necessary that . . . the trustee . . . was acting dishonestly, although this will usually be so. . . . Knowingly is better avoided as a defining ingredient of the principle and in the context of this principle the [*Baden v. Société Generale Pour Favoriser le Développement du Commerce et de L'industrie en France SA* [1993] 1 W.L.R. 509] . . . scale of knowledge is best forgotten." This clarifies the previous uncertainty over whether constructive knowledge (*i.e.* that the stranger ought to have known or mere negligence) was sufficient to make a stranger liable as a constructive trustee (see cases such as *Karak Rubber Co. Ltd v. Burden (No. 2)* [1972] 1 W.L.R. 602 and *Selangor United Rubber Estates v. Cradock (No. 3)* [1968] 2 All E.R. 1073). It is now necessary for the stranger to be dishonest in order for liability to arise—mere negligence or constructive knowledge being insufficient.

[2] Prior to this case, cases such as *Polly Peck International plc v. Nadir (No. 2)* [1992] 4 All E.R. 769, had already suggested that in order to make a stranger liable as a constructive trustee, there must be some dishonesty or want of probity on the part of the stranger. It was also necessary that the knowledge of the dishonest intent of the trustees be imputed on the stranger because liability as a constructive trustee was still on the basis of knowing assistance.

[3] Lord Nicholls suggested that the term "dishonesty" was to be judged objectively but with a subjective element taking into account the defendant's knowledge, experience, intelligence and reasons for his actions.

KEY PRINCIPLE: *Dishonesty is taken to mean conscious impropriety and would include closing one's eyes to the obvious.*

Lipkin Gorman v. Karpnale Ltd 1989

A partner in a firm of solicitors had used money in its client account for gambling. The firm *inter alia*, attempted to recover this money from the bank where the money had been deposited.

HELD: (CA) The bank was not liable as a constructive trustee unless it was also in breach of its contractual duty of care. As the bank had no reason to believe that there was a possibility that the money was being withdrawn in breach of trust, it was not liable. [1989] 1 W.L.R. 1340

Agip (Africa) Ltd v. Jackson 1991

The plaintiff signed a payment order in favour of a shipping company but the plaintiff's chief accountant fraudulently altered it by substituting Baker Oil Services Ltd ("Baker Oil"). Baker Oil was a company in which the first and third defendants were the sole directors and shareholders. The first and second defendants were partners in a firm of chartered accountants trading under the name of Jackson & Co. in the Isle of Man. The third defendant was an employee of the firm. The money was paid by the plaintiffs through its account with their bankers in Tunisia (Tunis Bank). The Tunis Bank instructed Citibank, their correspondents in New York, to credit Baker Oil's Bank, through the New York Clearing system. Jackson & Co. then ordered the bank to transfer the money to its account with the same branch of the bank. The money was subsequently transferred to a client account of the firm in the Isle of Man. Most of this money was subsequently transferred out on the instructions of clients. After the discovery of the fraud, the plaintiff sought to recover the money on the basis of money had and received at common law or on the basis that the defendants were constructive trustees.

HELD: (CA) In equity, the defendants were liable as constructive trustees because they assisted the chief accountant in his fraud. [1991] Ch. 547

COMMENTARY

[1] *Lipkin Gorman v. Karpnale Ltd* went on appeal to the House of Lords but this concerned the liability of the casino.
[2] In *AGIP (Africa) Ltd v. Jackson*, at first instance (reported at [1990] Ch. 265), Millet J. decided that the defendants were liable for knowing assistance (see now *Royal Brunei Airlines*

Sdn. Bhd. v. Tan) in a dishonest and fraudulent design. On the facts of the case, Millet J. held that this was dishonest because of their indifference to the state of affairs that existed. The Court of Appeal affirmed the decision of Millet J. on appeal.

KEY PRINCIPLE: *Liability on the basis of dishonest assistance requires the stranger to know of the existence of the trust or at least the facts giving rise to it.*

Brinks Ltd (formerly Brink's Mat Ltd) v. Abu Saleh (No. 3) 1995

As a result of a robbery at its warehouse at Heathrow, the plaintiff suffered a loss. The plaintiff issued proceedings against 57 defendants whom they believed had either been involved in the robbery or in laundering the money. The 13th defendant was alleged to have assisted her husband in laundering about £3 million by accompanying her husband on trips to Switzerland. Although she was aware that her husband was carrying the money as part of dishonest transaction, she thought that this was merely a tax evasion scheme.

HELD: (Ch.) The 13th defendant was not liable as a constructive trustee. Although she was aware that her husband was taking the money to Switzerland as part of a dishonest transaction, in order for her to be liable as a constructive trustee for dishonest assistance, she must have known of the existence of the trust or at least the facts giving rise to it. As she did not, she was not liable as a constructive trustee for dishonest assistance. *The Times*, October 23, 1995

COMMENTARY
The question that has arisen is whether this decision reintroduces the element of knowledge and constructive knowledge which the Privy Council in *Royal Brunei Airlines Sdn. Bhd. v. Tan* (above), was keen to avoid. This remains to be seen.

KEY PRINCIPLE: *Liability of a stranger as a constructive trustee can arise by virtue of receipt of trust property.*

Re Montague's Settlement Trusts 1987

Chattels which were subject to a resettlement were transferred to the 10th Duke of Manchester by trustees in breach of trust. Before they transferred the chattels, the trustees failed to ensure that the chattels were not subject to the resettlement. The 10th Duke sold some of the chattels. After the death of the 10th Duke, the plaintiff, who was the 11th Duke, commenced an action alleging, *inter alia*, that the 10th Duke held the chattels which were subject to the resettlement as a constructive trustee.

HELD: (Ch.) Although the trustees were in breach of their fiduciary duty in transferring the chattels to the 10th Duke, the 10th Duke was not liable as a constructive trustee. This was because at the relevant time when the chattels were transferred to him he did not know that the chattels were subject to a trust. [1987] 1 Ch. 264

COMMENTARY

A stranger could be liable as a constructive trustee where he or she has received trust property. In the case itself the 10th Duke was not liable as he did not know the items were transferred in breach of trust. Megarry V.-C. suggested (at 285) that ". . . knowledge . . . includes at least . . . actual knowledge that would have been acquired but for shutting one's eyes to the obvious, or wilfully and recklessly failing to make such inquiries as a reasonable and honest man would make; for in such cases there is a want of probity which justifies imposing a constructive trust". Other cases (see below) have, however, suggested that constructive notice is sufficient.

KEY PRINCIPLE: *In order for a stranger to be liable as a constructive trustee on the basis of knowing receipt, some authorities have suggested that constructive notice will suffice.*

Belmont Finance Corporation v. Williams Furniture Ltd (No. 2) 1980

A company received money from the illegal sale of a subsidiary company. The receiver of the subsidiary company subsequently claimed that the parent company was a constructive trustee of the proceeds of sale. This was on the basis that the illegal transaction occurred as a result of the director's breach of their fiduciary duties.

HELD: (CA) The parent company was a constructive trustee of the proceeds of sale on the basis of knowing receipt. [1980] 1 All E.R. 393

Eagle Trust plc v. SBC Securities Ltd 1992

The defendant agreed to underwrite a takeover bid initiated by the plaintiff. The chief executive of the defendant agreed to sub underwrite part of it. The plaintiff commenced an action to recover monies taken by the chief executive from the plaintiff for his own use. The plaintiff argued that the defendant was liable as a constructive trustee because the circumstances were such that it ought to have known or was put on enquiry that the chief executive would use the plaintiff's monies for his own purposes.

HELD: (Ch.) In order for the defendant to be liable as a constructive trustee of money received, it must be shown that it had actual knowledge of the breach of trust, or, had wilfully shut his eyes to the obvious or had wilfully and recklessly failed to make the type of inquiries which an honest and reasonable person would make. There was no evidence here that the defendant had the requisite knowledge and accordingly would not be liable as a constructive trustee. [1992] 4 All E.R. 488

COMMENTARY

Earlier cases such as *Belmont Finance Corporation v. Williams Furniture Ltd (No. 2)*, above, and *International Sales and Agencies Ltd v. Marcus* [1982] 3 All E.R. 551, suggested that something similar to constructive notice on the part of the stranger who received trust property would suffice, *i.e.* that the stranger knew or ought to have known that the property was subject to a trust. In *Re Montague's Settlement Trusts*, Megarry V.-C. appeared to have restricted this to actual knowledge. Other cases such as *Eagle Trust plc v. SBC Securities*, have required inferred knowledge as opposed to constructive notice. This could be explained on the basis that the case involved a commercial transaction where the doctrine of constructive notice in its strict conveyancing sense is not applied. See also *Cowan De Groot Properties Ltd v. Eagle Trust plc* [1992] 4 All E.R. 700.

KEY PRINCIPLE: *Knowledge on the part of an employee of the stranger who was its directing mind and will would suffice for the purpose of a constructive trust arising on the basis of knowing receipt.*

El Ajou v. Dollar Land Holdings plc 1994

The plaintiff placed substantial funds and securities under the control of his investment manager based in Geneva. The investment manager was bribed to invest the plaintiff's money in fraudulent share selling schemes operated by three Canadians through two Dutch companies. The proceeds of these schemes were invested in the first defendant. S was the Managing Director of a subsidiary of the first defendant. F was a Swiss fiduciary agent who acted for the Canadians but who was also the Chairman of the first defendant. The plaintiff subsequently discovered the fraud and commenced proceedings against the first defendant to recover the money received by it on the basis, *inter alia*, that the money was received with the knowledge that it represented the proceeds of fraud.

HELD: (CA) The first defendant would be liable as a constructive trustee. F had the *de facto* management and control of the relevant transactions and as such was its "directing mind and will". F's knowledge could be imputed to the first defendant and therefore a constructive trust on the basis of knowing receipt could be enforced. [1994] 2 All E.R. 685

Liability of Trustees' Agent

KEY PRINCIPLE: *A trustee's agent who innocently deals with trust funds is not liable as a constructive trustee.*

Williams-Ashman v. Price and Williams 1942

Trust funds paid into a firm of solicitors' bank account were subsequently invested in unauthorised investments on the instructions of the trustee.

HELD: (Ch.) The solicitor was not liable as a constructive trustee, as he had acted honestly on the instructions of the trustee. [1942] Ch. 219

COMMENTARY
Mara v. Browne [1896] 1 Ch. 199 was regarded as authority for the proposition that where the agent of the trustees acted

honestly, he or she is not accountable to the beneficiaries unless he has intermeddled with the duties of a trustee. Where the agent has not acted honestly or acts in a manner which he knows is contrary to the trust, he may be liable for having intermeddled in the trust.

Trusts of the Family Home

KEY PRINCIPLE: *In the absence of an expressed common intention as to the beneficial ownership in a property, the common intention can only be .inferred by direct financial contribution to the acquisition of the property.*

Lloyds Bank v. Rossett 1991

A husband and wife purchased a semi-derelict property with the husband's family trust providing the purchase price. The title to the property was put in the husband's name on the insistence of the trustees of the family trust. The purchasers were given access to the property before completion of the purchase. Renovation work was commenced with the wife doing some decorating and supervising the builders. Shortly after the work commenced, the husband obtained an overdraft facility for the renovation work. Upon default, possession proceedings were instituted. The wife claimed an interest in the property.

HELD: (HL) The wife's activities in respect of the property were not sufficient evidence on which an inference of common intention that the wife was to have a beneficial interest in the property could be drawn. In the absence of an expressed intention, the husband held the property for his own use and benefit. [1991] 1 A.C. 107

COMMENTARY
Lord Bridge (at 132–133) suggested that in the absence of an expressed common intention as to the beneficial interest in the property, it was doubtful that any conduct short of direct financial contribution to the purchase price would suffice. The position is that where there are direct financial contributions to the purchase price, for example by payment of the deposit or mortgage instalments, a beneficial interest in the property will arise. This beneficial interest will be held by way of a resulting trust (*Drake v. Whipp*, below). Where there is an expressed

common intention and the representee acted in reliance of it to his or her detriment, a beneficial interest could arise which would be held by way of a constructive trust (see below). See also *Halifax Building Society v. Brown* [1996] 1 F.L.R. 103.

KEY PRINCIPLE: *Where the owner of the property represents to the non-owning party that the latter was to have an interest in the property and the latter acted in reliance of it to his or her detriment, a constructive trust in favour of the latter may arise.*

Grant v. Edwards 1986

The plaintiff and first defendant moved into a house which was bought by the first defendant. At the time of the purchase, the first defendant told the plaintiff that her name would not be on the title because it would complicate her divorce proceedings. The house was put into the first defendant's and his brother's name. The first defendant paid the mortgage instalments with the plaintiff paying substantial household expenses. The parties separated in 1980 and the question arose as to the plaintiff's beneficial interest in the property.

HELD: (CA) A trust would be inferred where there was a common intention that both parties were to have a beneficial interest in the property and the non-owner had acted in reliance of this to his or her detriment. The excuse made by the first defendant gave rise to an inference of common intention that the plaintiff should have an interest in the property and since she had acted in reliance of it to her detriment by her substantial contribution to the household expenses, the plaintiff was entitled to a half share in the property. [1986] 1 Ch. 638

COMMENTARY
Likewise, in *Hammond v. Mitchell* [1991] 1 W.L.R. 1127, the court decided that the defendant had a beneficial interest in the family home in view of the express understanding that she was to have an interest in the property together with her contribution as a unpaid business assistant and the circumstances of the case.

KEY PRINCIPLE: *Where a constructive trust arises in favour of the person who acted in reliance of the representation of the owner of the property, the court can adopt a "broad brush" approach in deciding the extent of the parties' beneficial interest in the property.*

Drake v. Whipp 1996

The plaintiff and defendant bought a barn which was in the defendant's sole name. The plaintiff provided 40.1 per cent of the purchase price. The parties spent £129,536 on the property out of which the plaintiff contributed £13,000. The parties subsequently split up and the question arose as to the extent of the parties' interest in the property.

HELD: (CA) On the facts of the case, this was a case of constructive trust rather than resulting trust. In order for such a trust to arise, all that was needed was a common intention that the non-owning party should have a beneficial interest in the property and the latter had acted to his or her detriment in reliance of it. In constructive trust cases, the court can adopt a broad brush approach in determining the parties' share in the property. The plaintiff was entitled to a one third share in the property. [1996] 1 F.L.R. 826

COMMENTARY

[1] Gibson L.J. (at 827) suggested that the ". . . potent source of confusion, . . . has been suggestions that it matters not whether the terminology used is that of the constructive trust, to which the intention, actual or imputed, of the parties is crucial, or that of the resulting trust which operates as a presumed intention of the contributing party in the absence of rebutting evidence of actual intention". This decision is a welcome source of clarification as to when a constructive or resulting trust will arise.

[2] In the case of a resulting trust, the contributing party will be entitled to a beneficial interest to the extent of his or her contribution. In *Springette v. Defoe* [1992] 2 F.L.R. 388, a resulting trust arose and the plaintiff was held to be entitled to a 75 per cent share in the property as this represented the extent of her contribution. However, in *Midland Bank plc v. Cooke* [1995] 4 All E.R. 562, the Court of Appeal decided that where a resulting trust arose, it was permissible to look at the whole course of dealings and conduct between the parties

with regard to the ownership and occupation of the property. Although the contribution of the non-owning spouse amounted to 6.47 per cent only, the court found that she was entitled to a beneficial half interest in the property. This decision has been subject to much criticism and in light of *Drake v. Whipp* is open to doubt. Only in the case of the constructive trust, can the court adopt a broad brush approach and grant the non owning party a larger share in the property.

KEY PRINCIPLE: *An interest-free loan made by the non-owning party to the owner of the property may be taken into account in assessing the non-owning party's beneficial interest.*

Risch v. McFee 1990

The plaintiff who lived with the defendant made an interest-free loan to the latter but had not sought repayment of it.

HELD: (CA) The unpaid interest-free loan could be taken into account in assessing the plaintiff's beneficial interest in the property. *The Times,* July 6, 1990

COMMENTARY

Once the common intention that the plaintiff was to have a beneficial interest in the property was established, the court could take the interest free loan into account in assessing the plaintiff's beneficial interest.

Conveyance Induced by Fraud

KEY PRINCIPLE: *Where a conveyance has been induced by fraud, the transferee may have to hold the property on a constructive trust.*

Rochefoucauld v. Bousted 1897

The plaintiff agreed to sell some lands to the defendant who would hold it upon trust for the plaintiff. Without the plaintiff's consent, the defendant mortgaged the lands and subsequently became bankrupt. The plaintiff argued that the lands were held on trust for her.

HELD: (CA) The plaintiff was entitled to prove her claim by parol evidence despite the requirements of writing. Accordingly, since there was evidence that the lands were transferred subject to the trust in the plaintiff's favour, the defendant held the lands as trustee for the plaintiff. [1897] 1 Ch. 196

Bannister v. Bannister 1948

The defendant agreed to sell two cottages to the plaintiff subject to an agreement that she was to be allowed to live in one of them. The conveyance made no reference to the agreement. The plaintiff sought to evict the defendant.

HELD: (CA) A constructive trust arises to prevent a party from relying on the absolute nature of a conveyance for the purpose of defeating a beneficial interest in the property. The defendant was entitled to a declaration that the plaintiff held the house on a constructive trust during her life for her occupation for so long as she desired and accordingly the plaintiff was not entitled to evict her. [1948] 2 All E.R. 133

COMMENTARY

The Court of Appeal in *Rochefoucauld v. Bousted*, above, thought that they were enforcing an express rather than a constructive trust. However, later cases such as *Bannister v. Bannister*, above, have suggested that these situations give rise to a constructive trust. See also *Binions v. Evans* [1972] 2 All E.R. 70 and *Lyus v. Prowsa Developments Ltd* [1982] 2 All E.R. 953.

9. APPOINTMENT, RETIREMENT AND REMOVAL OF TRUSTEES

Introduction

The *Trusts of Land and Appointment of Trustees Act 1996* (*TLATA 1996*) has made several important changes to this area of the law. The changes are as follows.

- The beneficiaries, where they are of full age and capacity and absolutely entitled, and provided there is no other person nominated to appoint trustees, can give written

directions to the trustees to retire or appoint specified persons as trustees: section 19 of the *TLATA 1996*.
- The beneficiaries, provided they are of full age and capacity and absolutely entitled, can give a written direction for the appointment of a replacement trustee, where a trustee is incapable of acting as a trustee by reason of his metal state, and there is no person who is entitled and able to appoint a trustee in his place: section 20 of the *TLATA 1996*.

Appointment of Trustees

KEY PRINCIPLE: *A person who is resident abroad will be appointed as a trustee only where there are special circumstances.*

Re Whitehead's Will Trusts 1971
Trustees who were resident in the U.K. applied to court for permission to appoint new trustees who were resident in Jersey. The beneficiaries resided in Jersey.

HELD: (Ch.) There was no rule preventing the appointment of trustees who were resident abroad. However, the court would only do so rarely. It was appropriate in this case to allow such an appointment as the beneficiaries were resident abroad. [1971] 2 All E.R. 1334

KEY PRINCIPLE: *Where new trustees are appointed to replace existing trustees under section 36 of the Trustee Act 1925, the trustee being replaced need not be party to the decision.*

Re Stoneham Settlement Trusts 1952
One of two trustees of a family trust was out of the country for more than 12 months but was willing to continue as trustee. His co-trustee (who wished to retire) appointed new trustees in place of himself and the trustee who had been out of the country.

HELD: (Ch.) The trustee who had been out of the country did not need to have taken part in the decision. The appointment of the new trustees to replace existing trustees under section 36 of the *Trustee Act 1925* was valid. [1952] 2 All E.R. 694

COMMENTARY

The statutory power to appoint new trustees under section 36 of the *Trustee Act 1925* is available unless it has been expressly excluded. The power is given to persons who have been specifically nominated as persons having the power to appoint new trustees or where there is none, then to surviving and continuing trustees. Section 36(8) of the *Trustee Act 1925* provides that a continuing trustee includes the trustee who is refusing to act or a trustee who wishes to retire, so long as he is willing to appoint new trustees. Therefore, in this case, it was proper for the retiring trustee to appoint new trustees as replacement for himself and the trustee who was out of the country.

KEY PRINCIPLE: *Under section 36(1) of the Trustee Act 1925, the power of appointment can only be exercised to replace existing trustees, while, section 36(6) allows the appointment of additional trustees up to a maximum of four.*

Re Power's Settlement Trusts 1951

A tenant for life under a settlement was given the power to appoint new trustees under section 36 of the *Trustee Act 1925*. The tenant for life purported to appoint himself as an additional trustee.

HELD: (CA) The tenant for life cannot appoint himself as a trustee under the settlement. Under section 36(1) of the *Trustee Act 1925*, the power to appoint trustees is limited to the replacement of existing trustees. Under section 36(6) additional trustees can be appointed but this did not permit the person given the power to appoint new trustees to appoint himself. [1951] 2 All E.R. 513

KEY PRINCIPLE: *The court has the power to appoint new trustees under section 41 of the Trustee Act 1925.*

Re Tempest 1866

One of the trustees of a family settlement predeceased the testator. The persons with the power to appoint new trustees could not agree on a replacement. An application to court was made to appoint P. One of the beneficiaries opposed this because the proposed trustee was from a branch of the family with which the testator had not been on friendly terms.

HELD: (CA) In the circumstances of the case, P was not a proper person to be appointed as a trustee. (1866) LR 1 Ch. App. 485

COMMENTARY
In exercising its discretion, the court will take into account the wishes of the testator, where this is clear from the trust instrument or will. It would not normally appoint a person as a trustee where there is a risk that the appointed person may not serve the interests of all the beneficiaries by acting impartially. The court may need to take into account the reluctance of the surviving trustee to cooperate with the new trustee. However, the court suggested that in this case, this may be a ground for the removal of the existing trustee where he has acted unreasonably rather than as an argument against appointing the new trustee.

Disclaimer

KEY PRINCIPLE: *A person who has been appointed a trustee can avoid the office of trusteeship by disclaimer.*

Re Clout and Frewers Contract 1924
An executor trustee did not prove or act under the will for thirty years. He did not apply to take the legacy which the testator had left to him in the will.

HELD: (Ch.) The executor trustee's inaction amounted to a disclaimer by conduct. [1924] 2 Ch. 230

COMMENTARY
If the person appointed as a trustee wishes to avoid the office of a trustee, he should disclaim immediately and by deed, otherwise his actions may be taken as acceptance of the office of trusteeship: *Re Tyron* (1844) 7 Beav. 496. However, where the trustee has not done anything with the trust, his conduct can be taken as disclaimer. Once he is deemed to have accepted the office of trusteeship, he can no longer disclaim but can always retire from the trust under section 39 of the *Trustee Act 1925.*

Retirement of Trustees

KEY PRINCIPLE: *Where a trustee retired from the trust, he will not be liable for subsequent breaches of trust unless the breaches were contemplated by him when he retired.*

Head v. Gould 1898

H and C were the trustees of a marriage settlement, who were subsequently appointed trustees of a postnuptial settlement favouring the same beneficiaries. The trustees made various advances to the widow up to her full entitlement in some instances in breach of trust. The trustees retired and new trustees were appointed. After the appointment of the new trustees further breaches of trust occurred.

HELD: (Ch.) The trustees who retired would not be liable for the breach of trust committed by the present trustees. They would only be liable where it can be established that the breaches of trust were contemplated by them. It was not enough to show that the retirement facilitated the breach of trust. [1898] 2 Ch. 250

Removal of Trustees

KEY PRINCIPLE: *The court has an inherent jurisdiction to remove a trustee.*

Letterstedt v. Broers 1884

Several allegations of misconduct were made by a beneficiary against the trustee. The beneficiary asked for the trustee to be removed.

HELD: (PC) The court has a general duty to ensure the proper execution of the trust. As part of this duty, the court can remove a trustee if it is satisfied that the continuation of the trustee in office would impede the efficient administration of the trust. Accordingly, the trustee would be removed. (1884) 9 App. Cas. 371

COMMENTARY
Although the court has a statutory discretion to remove and replace a trustee under section 41 of the *Trustee Act 1925*, the court also has an inherent discretion to do so. The Privy

Council was reluctant to lay down general rules but merely stated that the interest of the beneficiary is paramount. It would ultimately depend on the circumstances of the case. The court was prepared to use its inherent jurisdiction to remove the trustees of the National Union of Mineworkers in *Clarke v. Heathfield* [1985] I.C.R. 606, where the trustees moved trust funds out of jurisdiction in order to avoid sequestration.

KEY PRINCIPLE: *The court will take into account all the circumstances of the case in deciding whether to remove a trustee.*

Re Wrightson 1908

The trustees admitted that a breach of trust had been committed. One of the issues was whether one of the trustees should be removed.

HELD: (Ch.) In the circumstances of the case, taking into account the fact that a large number of the beneficiaries wished the trustee to remain and the expense involved, the court would not order the removal of the trustee. [1908] 1 Ch. 789.

---

10. TRUSTEES' DUTIES

Fiduciary Duties

[a] The self dealing rule—the purchase of the trust estate

KEY PRINCIPLE: *Where a trustee purchases trust property, the sale can be set aside by the beneficiary.*

Wright v. Morgan 1926

The will stated that the property was to be offered for sale to the trustee-beneficiary at a price fixed by an independent valuer. The trustee-beneficiary assigned this option to purchase to another trustee who purchased the property at a price fixed by an independent valuer.

HELD: (PC) As there was a conflict of duty and interest, the sale would be set aside on the application of a beneficiary. [1926] A.C. 788

COMMENTARY
This rule had already been established in earlier cases such as *ex p. James* (1803) 8 Ves. 337 and *ex p. Lacey* (1802) 6 Ves. 265. To allow the trustee to purchase trust property would in fact be to allow the trustee to purchase the property from himself. There would be a conflict of interest and duty and, also, the trustee may have been aware of information relating to the property which others may not have been aware of. However, where there is an adequate lapse of time between the retirement and purchase, the purchase may be upheld: *Re Boles and British Land Co.'s Contract* [1902] 1 Ch. 244 (12-year gap).

KEY PRINCIPLE: *A trustee may purchase trust property where the trust instrument authorises it.*

Sargeant v. National Westminster Bank plc 1990

A testator appointed his wife and children as his executors and trustees under his will. The will authorised the purchase of the trust property by the trustees. Part of the estate consisted of several farms which he had let to his children to work on as a partnership before he died. The question arose as to whether the trustees could sell the freeholds of the farms to themselves.

HELD: (CA) As the trustees' rights pre-dated the will (by virtue of their tenancy of the farms), they had not put themselves in a position of conflict of interest and duty. Further, the express provision in the will allowing the trustees to purchase the trust property excluded the rule that a trustee could not purchase trust property. They could purchase the freeholds of the farm although they had a duty to obtain the best price. [1990] 61 P. & C.R. 518.

KEY PRINCIPLE: *The court may allow a trustee to purchase trust property in exceptional cases.*

Holder v. Holder 1968

An executor purported to renounce his executorship under a will after having carried out certain acts which amounted to intermeddling. Later, he purchased two farms owned by the estate, but of which he was the tenant of, at an auction. He paid a price which was probably higher than would have been paid by anyone else.

HELD: (CA) The sale would not be set aside. As the acts of administration which he had undertaken were minimal, and the knowledge which he acquired about the property was in his position as tenant rather than as an executor and he had not influenced the other executors, it was proper in the special circumstances of this case to allow the sale. [1968] Ch. 353

COMMENTARY

The executor did not take an active part in the administration of the estate, although he did some acts which amounted to intermeddling. It was conceded that these acts of intermeddling rendered the renunciation ineffective. However, Danckwerts L.J. suggested that this was a mistake and doubted whether the renunciation was rendered ineffective by the acts of intermeddling. It was felt that the acts of intermeddling were technical and trivial but since the concession was made, the executor technically remained as executor. However, since the evidence was that he took no part in arranging for the sale of the farms and had not influenced the other executor, it was proper to allow the sale.

[b] The Fair Dealing rule—the purchase of the beneficial interest

KEY PRINCIPLE: *A trustee may purchase the beneficial interest from a beneficiary provided there is a clear and distinct contract, and there is no fraud, concealment, or advantage taken of by the trustee of information obtained as a trustee.*

Morse v. Royal 1806

A beneficiary who sold his beneficial interest to a trustee subsequently regretted the sale when the price of the property went up. He applied for the sale to be set aside.

HELD: (Ch.) The sale would not be set aside. (1806) 12 Ves. 355

COMMENTARY
In *Tito v. Waddell (No. 2)* [1977] Ch. 106, Megarry V.-C. suggested that such a transaction is not voidable *ex debito justitiae*, but can be set aside by the beneficiary unless the trustee can show that he has taken no advantage of his position and has made full disclosure to the beneficiary, and the transaction is fair and honest.

[c] Competition against the trust

KEY PRINCIPLE: *A trustee is not allowed to set up a business in competition with the business carried out by the trust.*

Re Thomson 1930
Under the terms of the trust, the trustees were directed to look after the testator's business of a yacht broker. One of the trustees wished to set up a similar business.

HELD: (Ch.) The trustee would not be allowed to set up the business which would compete with the business of the trust as this would be a breach of his fiduciary duty. [1930] 1 Ch. 203

COMMENTARY
In such cases, there is the potential conflict of interest and duty. However, in the Irish case of *Moore v. M'glynn* (1894) 1 Ir.R. 74, the court refused to restrain an executor from competing with the estate but was prepared to remove the executor.

[d] The rule in Keech v. Sandford

KEY PRINCIPLE: *A trustee of a lease is not allowed to obtain a renewal of the lease for himself.*

Keech v. Sandford 1726
A trustee of a lease applied to the lessor for a renewal of the lease. The lessor refused to renew the lease in favour of the trust where the beneficiary was an infant. However, the lessor agreed to renew the lease in the trustee's own name.

HELD: (Ch) The trustee held the lease upon trust for the infant beneficiary and had to account for the profits. (1726) Sel. Cas. Ch. 61

COMMENTARY

The court refused to allow the trustee to retain the lease because of the potential conflict of interest and duty. There may be a disincentive for a trustee to secure a renewal of the lease for the trust where there was the possibility that he could obtain it for himself. This rule appears to extend to preventing the trustee from purchasing the freehold reversion: *Protheroe v. Protheroe* [1968] 1 W.L.R. 519. Where the person who obtains the renewal of the lease is not in a fiduciary position, the rule in *Keech v. Sandford* does not apply: *Re Biss* [1903] 2 Ch. 40.

[e] Remuneration

One of the consequences of the application of the rule that a trustee is not to profit from his position as a trustee is that a trustee is not entitled to remuneration for his work as a trustee. There are a number of exceptions to this rule. Trustees are, however, entitled to out of pocket expenses (section 30(2) of the *Trustee Act 1925*).

KEY PRINCIPLE: *Where a trustee acts on the behalf of the trust in his professional capacity as a solicitor, the trustee may charge for the costs of litigation.*

Craddock v. Piper 1850

One of the trustees who was a solicitor acted on behalf of himself and his co-trustees in two legal actions with regard to the trust property. In taxing the costs of the action, the Master refused to allow the trustee-solicitor's costs incurred for professional work.

HELD: (Ch.) The trustee-solicitor would be entitled to charge for the costs of litigation. (1850) 1 Mac. & G. 664

COMMENTARY

This rule has not been universally applied. In *Re Chalinder & Herrington* [1907] 1 Ch. 58, the court restricted this to work of a professional nature. The trustee-solicitor could not charge

for other work even though this may have been work normally
undertaken by a solicitor.

KEY PRINCIPLE: *The court has an inherent jurisdiction to
authorise remuneration in favour of the trustees.*

Boardman v. Phipps 1966
(See below).

HELD: (HL) The appellants had acted openly but had made
a mistake as to their rights. Their actions had been highly
beneficial to the trust and therefore it was appropriate to allow
remuneration for their work and skill. [1966] 3 All E.R. 721

Re Duke of Norfolk's Settlement Trusts 1981
One of the trustees of a settlement was a trust corporation. The
trust corporation subsequently became involved in extensive
redevelopment of trust property. This, together with the intro-
duction of Capital Transfer Tax, resulted in additional work for
the trustees. The trust corporation asked the court to authorise
remuneration for the services provided.

HELD: (CA) The court had an inherent jurisdiction to order
payment of remuneration to trustees where this would be of
benefit to the administration of the trust. In exercising this
jurisdiction, the court would have regard to the nature of the
trust, the expertise of the trustees, the remuneration requested,
the circumstances of the case and whether this would be in the
best interests of the trust.[1981] 3 All E.R. 220

COMMENTARY
[1] In the exercise of the court's inherent jurisdiction to award
remuneration, the court would balance, on the one hand, the
fact that the office of a trustee is normally gratuitous and on
the other hand, to ensure that the trust was properly administered. Ultimately, the question is whether it would be in the
best interests of the trust. In *Foster v. Spencer* [1996] 2 All
E.R. 672, the court was prepared to exercise its inherent
jurisdiction to order remuneration for the trustees.
[2] Where the court appoints a trust corporation as a trustee,
it has the power to authorise remuneration: section 42 of the
Trustee Act 1925.

KEY PRINCIPLE: *Where the trustee receives Director's fees or salary as a result of being appointed to the Board of Directors by virtue of the trust's share holding, he may have to account to the trust for the monies received.*

Re Francis 1905

The trustees became directors as a result of the trust's share holding in the company. The issue arose as to whether the trustees had to account for the remuneration received.

HELD: (Ch.) Applying the rule that trustees cannot profit from their position as trustees, the trustees were under a duty to account to the trust for their remuneration. (1905) 74 L.J. Ch. 198

Re Dover Coalfield Extension Ltd. 1907

Shares owned by D Company in K Company were transferred to one of its directors in order to qualify to be on the Board of Directors. The director executed a declaration of trust in respect of those shares.

HELD: (CA) The remuneration received by the director from his directorship in K Company was not profit received from use of property owned by D Company. Therefore, the director was under no liability to account. [1908] 1 Ch. 65

COMMENTARY
[1] Notwithstanding the benefits of having the trustee on the Board of Directors of a company, the trustees may have to account to the trust for monies received from that position. In *Re Dover Coalfield Extension Ltd* the court decided that the director could retain the fees because he had been appointed a director before the shares was transferred to him. The cases are not entirely consistent. In *Re Macadam* [1945] 2 All E.R. 664, trustees who held directorships in a company on the trust's behalf were held liable to account to the trust.
[2] Where it is clear that the testator intended the trustee to retain the directors' fees, the trustee may do so: *Re Llewellin's Will Trusts* [1949] Ch. 225.

[f] Trustees or fiduciaries cannot make a profit from that capacity.

KEY PRINCIPLE: *A trustee or fiduciary cannot make a profit from his position as trustee even though the trust may have declined or was unable to make use of the opportunity.*

Boardman v. Phipps 1966

The trust held some shares in a private company. Boardman, who was the solicitor for the trust and one of the trustees wanted new directors to be appointed at the company. This failed and it was decided that the only way to make the company profitable was to take a controlling interest in the company. The trust was unable to acquire further shares in the company. Therefore, with the trustees' consent, Boardman and one of the beneficiaries acquired a controlling interest in the company and made it profitable. This benefited the trust, Boardman and the beneficiary. One of the other beneficiaries claimed that Boardman and the beneficiary had to account for the profits which they made.

HELD: (HL) Boardman and the other beneficiary by their actions were put in a fiduciary position. As such, any information they obtained about the company was acquired in that capacity. Therefore, they were not entitled to keep the profit acquired by them and had to account as constructive trustees to the trust for those profits. [1966] 3 All E.R. 721.

Regal (Hastings) Ltd v. Gulliver 1942

A company wanted to acquire the leases of two cinemas. In order to do this, it set up a subsidiary company. The lessor refused to grant the leases unless the capital of the subsidiary company was fully paid up. The parent company did not have the funds to do this. The directors of the parent company bought some of the shares in the subsidiary company. The leases were granted and when the subsidiary company was subsequently sold, both the parent company and the directors made a profit.

HELD: (HL) The directors had to account for the profits which they made from the sale of the subsidiary company notwithstanding that the directors had acted bona fide. [1942] 1 All E.R. 378

COMMENTARY

In *Boardman v. Phipps*, it was clear that there was no question of bad faith on the part of Boardman and the beneficiary.

Linked with the fact that the profit resulted from their hard work, the court decided that they were entitled remuneration for the work. Their Lordships further suggested that they could have protected themselves by obtaining consent. Another important point to note is that Boardman and the beneficiary were not trustees but had by their actions put themselves in a position whereby they owed a fiduciary duty to the trust.

KEY PRINCIPLE: *The court has the discretion to authorise a scheme where there is a conflict between the trustees' duty and their interests.*

Re Drexel Burnham Lambert U.K. Pension Plan 1995

The plaintiffs were the trustees of a pension scheme. The first defendant was the principal employer until it was wound up in 1990. The trustees were also beneficiaries under the scheme. The administrators of the first defendant gave notice that the pension scheme should terminate in July 1990 resulting in a substantial surplus. The rules of the scheme gave the trustees the absolute discretion to apply the surplus to secure further benefits within the limits set out in the rules of the scheme and any further balance was to be apportioned among the first defendant and other participating employers. The trustees sought directions from the court. The question arose as to whether the court could give directions in respect of a proposed scheme by the trustees who were beneficiaries as well.

HELD: (Ch.) The rule that a trustee must not be in position whereby his duty as trustee conflicted with his own interest did not necessarily involve questions of wrongdoing or morality. However, the rules of equity were adaptable with various exceptions to the rules. The court, therefore, had jurisdiction to give directions as to the exercise of the trustees' discretion even though the trustees were in a position of conflict. As the proposed scheme had commended itself to the court and had been examined by counsel and solicitors, the court allowed the trustees to adopt the scheme. [1995] 1 W.L.R. 32

COMMENTARY
The court accepted that there may circumstances where it may be proper to allow a proposal even though the trustees

may be in a position of conflict. The court recognised that the general rule that trustees must not put themselves in a position of conflict between their interest and duty is riddled with exceptions and relaxations of the rule.

[g] Where the trust has a controlling interest in a company or business.

KEY PRINCIPLE: *Where the trust owns a controlling interest in a company, the trustees will be expected to take an active part in the management of the company.*

Re Lucking's Will Trusts 1967
(See Chap. 11).

HELD: (Ch.) Trustees who hold a majority share holding in a company on trust should take more care than a normal shareholder and should ensure that they have adequate information regarding the running of the business.[1967] 3 All E.R. 726

Bartlett v. Barclays Bank Trust Co. Ltd (No. 1) 1980
(See Chap. 13).

HELD: (Ch.) It was improper for the professional trustee to confine itself merely to the receipt of the company's accounts and to attendance at general meetings. The trustee should have taken a more active role, which if it had, would have enabled it to prevent speculative investments. [1980] 1 Ch. 515

Duty to Invest

KEY PRINCIPLE: *Where the trustees have been given an express power of investment, the extent of that power is a matter of construction.*

Re Harari's Settlement Trusts 1949
A settlor recited the transfer of some securities to trustees in his settlement. In the settlement, he directed the trustees to hold the investments but had the power to retain it in its present form or may realise the investments and invest in such investments as they may deem fit.

HELD: (Ch.) On a true construction of the settlement, the trustees had power, under the express power of investment, to invest in any investments they deem fit. [1949] 1 All E.R. 430

Re Wragg 1919

Trustees of a will were given the power to invest in " . . . stocks, shares and securities or other investments of whatsoever nature and wheresoever as his trustees should in their absolute and uncontrolled discretion think fit with the like power of varying such investments to the intent that his trustees should have the same full and unrestricted powers of investing and transposing investments as if they were absolutely entitled".

HELD: (Ch.) The trustees had the power to invest in the purchase of real property. [1919] 2 Ch. 58

COMMENTARY

Where an express power of investment is concerned, the extent of the power is a matter of interpretation. In *Re Power* [1947] Ch. 572, where the trustees were given an express power to invest the trust fund including the purchase of freehold land, the court held that the trustees could only purchase freehold land as an investment and not purchase a home to allow the beneficiaries to live there rent-free. This is now subject to section 12 of the *Trusts of Land and Appointment of Trustees Act 1996*. This, where relevant. provides that the trustees of land have the power to allow the beneficiaries to reside in the property if the purposes of the trust include making the land available for the occupation by the beneficiary or beneficiaries OR (*my emphasis*) the land is held by the trustees so as to be available for occupation. Where two or more beneficiaries are entitled to occupy the property under section 12, the trustees have the power under section 13 to exclude or restrict the entitlement of anyone or more (but not all) of them.

KEY PRINCIPLE: *In making investment decisions, trustees are under a duty to take such care as ordinary prudent persons would take if they were minded to make an investment in favour of persons whom they felt morally bound to provide.*

Learoyd v. Whiteley 1886

Trust funds were invested by the trustees in a 5 per cent mortgage of a freehold brickfield with buildings, machinery, and plant. This was on the advice of competent valuers that the property was good security for the loan. The trustees acted on this advice without any further enquiries. The report failed to state whether the valuation was based on the property being a going concern and failed to distinguish between the value of the land and the buildings and machinery. The borrower defaulted on the loan and the security proved inadequate.

HELD: (HL) The trustees had failed to act with ordinary prudence and therefore were liable to repay the loan with interest at 4 per cent from the date of the last payment. (1887) 12 App. Cas. 727

Nestle v. National Westminster Bank plc 1993

In 1986 the plaintiff became entitled to the residue of her grandfather's estate. The estate was originally worth £54,000 in 1922 when her grandfather died. The defendant was the trustee of the estate. When the plaintiff became entitled, the estate was worth £269,203. The plaintiff alleged that the estate would have been worth more if the defendant had managed the trust with proper care. She alleged that the defendant had failed in their duty to conduct periodic reviews of the investments, failed to balance the interests of the remainderman and the life tenant and failed to diversify the investments.

HELD: (CA) Although the defendant has failed to appreciate the scope of its powers of investment, and had failed to conduct a periodic review of the investments, this was not enough to give the plaintiff a remedy. The plaintiff had to show that the decisions made by the defendant were decisions which a reasonable prudent trustee would not have made. Therefore, the plaintiff failed to establish that the defendant had committed a breach of trust.[1993] 1 W.L.R. 1260

COMMENTARY

In *Learoyd v. Whiteley* (reported at (1886) 33 Ch. D. 347), Lindley L.J. stated (at 355) that " . . . [t]he duty of a trustee is not to take such care only as a prudent man would take if he had only himself to consider; the duty rather is to take such care as an ordinary man would take if he were minded to make an investment for the benefit of other people for whom he felt morally bound to provide".

KEY PRINCIPLE: *The trustees have to put aside their personal views when investing trust property.*

Cowan v. Scargill 1984

Five out of the 10 trustees of the Mineworkers' Pension Scheme refused to approve an investment plan unless it prohibited an increase in foreign investments, provided for the withdrawal of existing foreign investments and prohibited investments in energies which competed with coal. The other five trustees sought a declaration as to whether the refusal to adopt the investment plan amounted to a breach of trust.

HELD: (Ch.) The duty of the trustees was to act in the best interests of the beneficiaries and since the purpose of the trust was to provide financial benefits, the fund had to be invested so as to yield the best returns both in terms of income and capital appreciation. The trustees' personal views or moral reservations were irrelevant to the choice of investments except that in exceptional cases, the view of the beneficiaries may be taken into account. Accordingly, the trustees who refused to approve the investment plan would be in breach of trust. [1984] 3 W.L.R. 501

Harries v. The Church Commissioners for England 1992

The plaintiffs sought a declaration that in the management of the trust funds of the Church of England, the Church Commissioners were obliged to have regard to the object of promoting the Christian faith through the established Church of England and may not act contrary to that objective.

HELD: (Ch.) Where charitable trustees held investments for a trust, their duty of furthering the purposes of the trust would normally require them to get the best possible returns from the investments consistent with commercial prudence. As the object of the trust funds held by the Church Commissioners was the provision of financial assistance to the clergy of the Church of England, their policy of excluding investments which would be offensive to some in the church was proper since there were alternative investments of a suitable nature. The Commissioners were however, entitled to reject a more restrictive policy and divergent views on moral questions which would be detrimental financially to the trust even though this might conflict with the objects of the trust. The declaration was refused. [1992] 1 W.L.R. 1241.

COMMENTARY
Where the object of the trust is financial provision for the beneficiaries, the trustees have to adopt an investment policy which would provide the best returns to the trust. Even though they may have personal or moral beliefs, these have to be set aside where it would be financially detrimental to the trust. In some circumstances, they may take into account the particular views of the beneficiaries but as was suggested in *Cowan v. Scargill*, this would only be in exceptional cases.

KEY PRINCIPLE: *In appropriate cases, the court may authorise an extension of the trustees' investment powers.*

Trustees of the British Museum v. Attorney-General 1984

The court had in 1960 approved a scheme of investment which enabled trust fund belonging to the British Museum to keep pace with inflation until 1983. As a result of cuts in public funding and steep rises in costs of acquiring museum pieces, this was no longer possible. The trustees applied to the court for an extension of their investment powers.

HELD: (Ch.) In light of the need to keep up with inflationary pressures and cuts in public funding, and the fact that this large fund was well-managed and well-supervised, the court would give approval for an investment scheme which went beyond that permitted by the *Trustee Investments Act 1961*. [1984] 1 All E.R. 337

Mason v. Farbrother 1983
(See Chap. 12).

HELD: (Ch) The court could substitute wider investment powers under section 57 of the *Trustee Act 1925* where it would be expedient for the management and administration of trust property. [1983] 2 All E.R. 1078

COMMENTARY

In *Re Kolb's Will Trusts* [1961] 3 W.L.R. 1034, the court stated that there must be special circumstances before the court would be prepared to extend the trustees' power of investments beyond that permitted by the *Trustee Investments Act 1961*. In *Trustees of the British Museum v. Attorney-General*, Megarry V.-C. decided that *Re Kolb's Will Trusts* should no longer be followed and therefore there was no necessity to establish special circumstances in order for the extension of the investment powers to be given. General economic changes would be adequate. Megarry V.-C. suggested that *Re Kolb's Will Trusts* was correct at the time, having been decided shortly after the 1961 Act but the changes in the last 20 years would justify a departure from that decision. The approach in *Trustees of the British Museum v. Att.-Gen.* has been followed in later cases such as *Steel v. Wellcome Custodian Trustees* [1988] 1 W.L.R. 167 where the court granted an extension of the powers of investment after taking into account the size of the fund, the eminence of the trustees, and the provisions for taking advice.

Duty to balance the interests of present and future beneficiaries

KEY PRINCIPLE: *Trustees are under a duty to balance the interests of present and future beneficiaries.*

Howe v. Earl of Dartmouth 1802

By his will dated October 25, 1774, the testator left all his realty and personalty to his wife for life and thereafter to other persons in succession. Part of his personalty consisted of bank stock, long and short annuities. The stock and annuities were subsequently sold by the trustees and authorised investments purchased in its place.

HELD: (Ch.) It was proper for the trustees to sell the bank stock and the annuities and convert them into authorised investments.(1802) 7 Ves. 137

COMMENTARY

The principle established by this case is that trustees are under a duty to sell unauthorised and wasting or hazardous investments and reversionary interests and reinvest them in authorised investments. In *Howe v. Earl of Dartmouth*, the bank stock was an unauthorised investment whilst the annuities were regarded as a wasting asset. This is to ensure that the interests of the future and present beneficiaries are protected. The rule in *Howe v. Earl of Dartmouth* is subject to a contrary intention in the will. Further, if the trustees are directed not to sell any of the investments or are given the discretion whether or not to sell the investments, this rule does not apply: *Re Pitcairn* [1896] 2 Ch. 199.

KEY PRINCIPLE: *Where the rule in Howe v. Earl of Dartmouth applies and there is a delay in the sale of the unauthorised, wasting or hazardous investments, the trustees may have to apportion the income from those investments between present and future beneficiaries.*

Re Fawcett 1940

Residuary estate was left by a testatrix on trust for the trustees to invest and to divide the income equally among her nephews and nieces and after their death, to divide it equally among their children upon them attaining the age of 21. Part of the residuary estate consisted of unauthorised investments.

HELD: (Ch.) The rule in *Howe v. Earl of Dartmouth* applied. Where the unauthorised investments remained unsold at the end of one year after the testatrix's death, the life tenants were entitled to interest at the rate of 4 per cent from the date of death till the sale of the unauthorised investments. The excess income from the unauthorised investments after the interest had been paid to the life tenants were to be invested in authorised investments. [1940] 1 Ch. 402

11. TRUSTEES' POWERS

Maintenance

Section 31 of the *Trustee Act 1925* gives the trustees the power to provide maintenance to the beneficiaries from the income. For the power to be exercisable, the legacy or devise must carry intermediate income. This is subject to section 175 of the *Law of Property Act 1925*, which provides that where there is a specific contingent gift of personalty or realty, the gift will carry the intermediate income except where the income is expressly disposed of.

KEY PRINCIPLE: *Section 175 of the Law of Property Act 1925 has no application to a contingent pecuniary legacy and therefore the intermediate income is generally not available for maintenance.*

Re Raine 1929

Two pecuniary legacies were bequeathed by the testator contingently upon the legatees reaching the age of 21. The question arose as to whether section 175 of the *Law of Property Act 1925* applied to contingent pecuniary legacies and whether the legacies carried the intermediate income.

HELD: (Ch.) Section 175 of the *Law of Property Act 1925* has no application to a contingent pecuniary legacy. Section 175 refers only to bequests or devises of realty or personalty and makes no reference to legacies. As such, the pre-1925 law will apply to legacies in which contingent pecuniary legacies did not carry the intermediate income. [1929] 1 Ch. 716

COMMENTARY
The court emphasised that there were exceptions to the general rule where the legacy would carry the intermediate income. These are where the testator:

- has shown an intention that the legatee should be maintained (*Re Churchill* [1909] 2 Ch. 431);
- was the father or stood in *loco parentis* to the infant legatee (*Re Boulter* [1918] 2 Ch. 40);
- has directed that the legacy be set aside as a separate fund for the benefit of the legatee (*Re Dickson* (1885) 29 Ch.D. 537).

KEY PRINCIPLE: *A deferred gift of realty does not carry the intermediate income, and thus the trustees cannot use the statutory power of maintenance.*

Re McGeorge 1963

The testator left property to his daughter under his will but directed that the gift was not to take effect until his wife died. The daughter upon attaining the age of 21, applied for the income to be paid over to her.

HELD: (Ch.) The daughter was not entitled to the income from the property as the gift was a deferred gift of realty and not a contingent gift. Section 175 of the *Law of Property Act 1925* did not apply. The gift did not therefore carry the intermediate income. [1963] 1 Ch. 544

COMMENTARY

A deferred gift of realty is different from a contingent gift. Only in the case of the latter does the gift carry the intermediate income. Section 175 of the *Law of Property Act 1925* refers to contingent gifts and not deferred gifts, therefore, the section had no application in this case. The trustees do not have the power of maintenance in the case of a deferred gift.

KEY PRINCIPLE: *A deferred bequest of residuary personalty or realty does not carry the intermediate income.*

Re Oliver 1947

The testator left his two daughters a deferred vested bequest of his residuary estate. The issue was whether the bequest carried the intermediate income.

HELD: (Ch.D.) A vested deferred bequest of the residuary estate does not carry the intermediate income. [1947] 2 All E.R. 161

COMMENTARY

Whilst it is clear that a deferred vested devise of residuary realty and personalty does not carry the intermediate income, the position with respect to deferred contingent devise of residuary realty is unclear. There is no authority on this point but it is argued that the position should be the same in that the devise should not carry the intermediate income. In the case of a deferred contingent bequest of residuary personalty, the bequest does not normally carry the intermediate income: *Re Geering* [1964] Ch. 136

KEY PRINCIPLE: *The statutory power of maintenance can be excluded either expressly or by a contrary intention.*

Re Turner's Will Trusts 1937

One fifth of the testator's residue estate was given to the children of his late son living at his death, who should have reached or would thereafter reach the age of 28. The will gave the trustees the power to use the income for the education of the grandchildren and to accumulate the surplus. There were three grandchildren, one of whom died before reaching 28. At the date of his death, his share of the accumulated income amounted to £3,421. If this sum passed to his estate, this would have resulted in a substantial increase of the estate duty payable. Those entitled to his estate argued that the accumulated income should go to the other two grandchildren.

HELD: (CA) Although section 31(1)(ii) of the *Trustee Act 1925* required the income to be paid to a beneficiary who had attained the age of 18 but had not yet received a vested interest in the income, section 69(2) of the *Trustee Act 1925* allows section 31 to be expressly or impliedly excluded. Where a contrary intention is present in the trust instrument, this would be taken to have impliedly excluded the operation of the statutory power of maintenance. As the statutory power of maintenance had been impliedly excluded, the accumulated income did not go to the deceased grandchild's estate but to the other two grandchildren. [1937] Ch. 15

COMMENTARY

The statutory power of maintenance is impliedly excluded where there is an inconsistent provision in the trust instrument or where there is an express power of maintenance inconsistent with the statutory power. See also *Re Ransome's Will Trusts* [1957] 1 All E.R. 690 and *Re Erskine's Settlement Trusts* [1971] 1 W.L.R. 162.

Advancement

The trustees may have the power to make an advancement to beneficiaries for their advancement or benefit, either under the terms of the trust instrument or section 32 of the *Trustee Act 1925*.

KEY PRINCIPLE: *Although section 32(2) of the Trustee Act 1925 restricts the application of section 32 to trust property which is personalty, where the beneficiary intends to acquire realty which is already subject to the trust, the trustees can convey that realty to him rather than to give him capital money.*

Re Collard's Will Trusts 1961

The trust instrument provided that the trustees had the statutory power of advancement except for the purpose of acquiring a share or interest in any business. The beneficiary was working on a farm which was owned by the trust. The trustees wished to convey the farm to the beneficiary for the purpose of avoiding estate duty.

HELD: (Ch.D.) In the circumstances of the case, the trustees could transfer the farm to beneficiary in the exercise of their statutory power of advancement. As the trustees could have given the beneficiary capital moneys in order to purchase the farm, there was no objection to the direct conveyance of the farm to the beneficiary. Further, the purpose of the advancement was to avoid estate duty and not to further the beneficiary's business interest. [1961] 1 All E.R. 821

COMMENTARY

The court was able to reach the conclusion that the transfer of the farm to the beneficiary was not an acquisition of a business interest because the beneficiary already had security of tenure as tenant of the farm under the *Agricultural Holdings Act 1948*. Therefore, the acquisition of the freehold reversion did not give the beneficiary any added advantage as a farmer.

KEY PRINCIPLE: *The statutory power of advancement must be made for the advancement or benefit of the beneficiary.*

Pilkington v. I.R.C. 1964

The trustees wished to use their statutory power of advancement to settle part of the trust fund on new trusts primarily to avoid estate duty.

HELD: (HL) The term "advancement or benefit" meant any use of the capital money which would improve the material situation of the beneficiary. There was nothing in section 32 which prevented the creation of new settlement nor which excluded tax avoidance from being a benefit. It did not matter that the new settlement might provide an incidental benefit to other members of the beneficiary's family. However, the new settlement infringed the rule against remoteness of vesting and would therefore not be allowed. [1964] A.C. 612

COMMENTARY

Where the trustees are given the power of advancement either expressly or by statute, the trustees must ensure that the exercise of their discretionary power is for "the advancement or benefit" of the beneficiary. The term advancement is normally taken to mean making a permanent provision for the beneficiary by for example setting him up in business or buying him a home (*Re Williams' Will Trusts* [1953] 1 All E.R. 536). The term benefit has a wider meaning. In *Lowther v. Bentinck* (1874) L.R. 19 E.Q. 166, it was taken to include the discharge of a beneficiary's debts.

KEY PRINCIPLE: *A donation to charity giving rise to a temporal or spiritual benefit is to be regarded as being for the benefit of the beneficiary.*

Re Clore's Settlement Trusts 1966

A settlement was set up for the benefit of the settlor's son and daughter in equal shares on trust to accumulate the income whilst they were minors. The income was then to be paid to them directly until they attained the age of 30. Thereafter, the capital and income was to be held on trust for the son and daugther absolutely or their children if they should die under the age. The trustees had power to advance up to two-thirds of the presumptive or vested share in the trust fund to the beneficiaries. After the settlor's son attained the age of 21, the trustees sought to pay one seventh of the son's presumptive share to a charity in the exercise of their power of advancement.

HELD: (Ch.) It was a proper exercise of the power of advancement to make appropriate donations to charity on behalf of the beneficiary. As this was in discharge of a moral obligation to make donations to charity, this would be regarded as a benefit. [1966] 1 W.L.R. 955

COMMENTARY

The requirement of the advancement being for the advancement or benefit of the beneficiary is not restricted to financial or material benefit.

KEY PRINCIPLE: *Under section 32 of the Trustee Act 1925, the consent of the person with a prior life or other interest, whether vested or contingent, who must be in existence and of full age, has to be obtained in writing before the advancement can be made.*

Henley v. Wardell 1988

By Clause 10 of his will, the testator gave the trustees a power of advancement "to the intent that the powers given to trustees by section 32 of the *Trustee Act 1925* shall be enlarged so as to permit my trustees in their absolute and uncontrolled discretion to advance at any time the whole of any expectant or presumptive share to any of my children . . .". The issue was whether this avoided the need to obtain the consent of the person with a prior life or other interest.

HELD: (Ch.) The consent of the person with a prior life or other interest had to be obtained in writing in accordance with section 32. Clause 10 had the effect of enlarging the share which the trustees could advance to the beneficiary but did not remove the requirement to obtain the consent of the person with a prior interest. *The Times*, January 29, 1988

COMMENTARY

The court stated that Clause 10 could not be construed so as to exclude the need to obtain the consent in writing of the person with a prior life or other interest. Presumably, if the clause was worded properly, the need to obtain the consent in writing of the prior life interest could be excluded.

KEY PRINCIPLE: *In exercising their power of advancement, the trustees must ensure that purpose for which the advancement was made is actually carried out.*

Re Pauling's Settlement 1964

A marriage settlement gave the trustee a power to make advances to the children of the marriage for their advancement or benefit. Between 1948 and 1954, the trustee made a number of advances to the children, who on some of the occassions obtained independent legal advice purportedly for the children's benefit or advancement. However, some of the advances were used by their parents for their own benefit including the purchase of a family home in the Isle of Man in the parents' name. The children sued the trustee for breach of trust.

HELD: (CA) The power of advancement is a fiduciary power and therefore the trustee must weigh the benefit of the advancement against the rights of those who might become entitled under the settlement. If the circumstances warranted it, the trustee was under a duty to ensure that the advancement was used for the benefit for which it was intended and not allow the person to whom the advancement was made the freedom to spend it in any way he chose. [1964] 1 Ch. 303

COMMENTARY

The obligation on the trustee to ensure that the advancement is used for the purpose for which it is intended depends on the reliability of the beneficiary and the circumstances of the case. Where the beneficiary is reliable and the trustee is satisfied that the beneficiary will use the advance for the stated purpose, the trustee can leave the money in the hands of the beneficiary. However, if some doubt exists then the trustee has to ensure that the money is used for the purpose for which the advancement was made and not leave the money in the hands of the beneficiary.

KEY PRINCIPLE: *Where the beneficiary has received his one half of his vested or presumptive share in the trust fund, the trustees are not allowed to make further advances to him where the remainder of the fund has increased in value.*

Re Marquess of Abergavenny's Estate Act Trusts 1981

The trustees of a trust fund advanced one half of the beneficiary's share to him in the exercise of their power of advancement. The remainder of the trust fund subsequently increased in value. The question arose as to whether the trustees could make further advances to the beneficiary.

HELD: (Ch.) The trustees could not make further advances to the beneficiary as they had already advanced one half of the beneficiary's share to him. [1981] 2 All E.R. 643

COMMENTARY
The point here is that where the power of advancement has been exhausted, even though the remainder of the trust fund increases in value, the trustees cannot make further advancements to the same beneficiary.

KEY PRINCIPLE: *The statutory power of advancement can be excluded by a contrary intention.*

Re Evans's Settlement 1967
A trust instrument gave the trustees the power to advance up to £5,000.

HELD: (Ch.) The effect of this was to impliedly exclude the statutory power of advancement. [1967] 1 W.L.R. 1294

COMMENTARY
Section 69(2) of the *Trustee Act 1925* provides that the powers conferred on trustees by the Act can be expressly excluded by a contrary intention. This would include the statutory power of advancement. In addition, the statutory power of advancement will be impliedly excluded where the trust instrument is inconsistent with the statutory power of advancement.

Delegation and Liability for Delegatee

KEY PRINCIPLE: *At common law, the trustees may appoint a broker or solicitor to do that which, in the ordinary course of business, other people would employ brokers and solicitors to do and would not be liable if the broker or solicitor turns out to be dishonest.*

Speight v. Gaunt 1883

The trustee employed a broker to acquire shares on behalf of the trust. The trustee gave the broker money for this purpose. However, the broker used the money for his own purposes and subsequently became insolvent. The beneficiaries sued the trustee claiming that they had breached their fiduciary obligation be giving the money to the broker, although this was in accordance with established practice.

HELD: (HL) That the trustee was not liable to the beneficiary for the loss of the trust funds caused by the broker's dishonesty. (1883) 9 A.C. 1

COMMENTARY
Prior to the *Trustee Act 1925*, the trustees had a power to appoint agents like solicitors and brokers to carry out some of their duties if this was what ordinary persons would have done. If the agent turned out to be dishonest, the trustees would not be liable if they had followed the usual and regular course adopted by ordinary men in the course of business.

KEY PRINCIPLE: *In exercising the power to delegate certain functions to an agent, the trustees must act as an ordinary prudent man of business and employ the correct agent for the purpose.*

Wyman v. Paterson 1900

The trustees left part of the trust fund in the hands of their law agent and allowed it to be left uninvested for six months. The law agent then became insolvent and most of the money was unrecoverable. The beneficiaries sued the trustees for breach of trust, claiming wrongful delegation.

HELD: (HL) The trustees were in breach of trust as they should not have left the money in the hands of the law agent and treated him as a broker. It was not a question of vicarious liability. The trustees were not entitled to employ the law agent for the purpose of investing the trust funds. [1900] A.C. 271

COMMENTARY
In exercising their power to appoint an agent, the trustees must ensure that they appoint the appropriate agent. On the facts of the case, to appoint a law agent as a broker was an

improper exercise of their powers. In the earlier case of *Fry v. Tapson* (1884) 28 Ch.D. 268, the court decided that the trustees must appoint agents to do the normal type of work undertaken by that type of agent, otherwise it would be regarded as an improper delegation.

KEY PRINCIPLE: *A trustee is liable under section 30 of the Trustee Act 1925 for the default or misconduct of an agent only if the trustee has been guilty of wilful default.*

Re Vickery 1931

The defendant was the sole executor of the testatrix's estate who employed a solicitor to wind up the estate. Unbeknown to the defendant, the solicitor had previously been suspended from practice. The trust funds included money in a Post Office Savings Bank deposit account and savings certificates. The relevant savings book and savings certificates were deposited with the solicitor. Three months later, the first plaintiff, who was one of the beneficiaries, told the defendant of the solicitor's previous suspension from practice. Subsequently, the first plaintiff asked the defendant to employ another solicitor but the defendant failed to do so. The solicitor then absconded and some monies were unrecoverable. The plaintiffs sought a declaration that the defendant was guilty of breach of trust by allowing the monies to be retained by the solicitor. The defendant relied on section 23 of the *Trustee Act 1925* as his defence.

HELD: (Ch.) An executor who had employed an agent to receive monies belonging to the estate under section 23 of the *Trustee Act 1925*, would not be liable if the money is lost through the agent's misconduct, unless the executor is guilty of wilful default in accordance with section 30 of the *Trustee Act 1925*. On the facts of the case, the defendant was only guilty of an error of judgment, which, as the losses were due to the solicitor's dishonesty, did not amount to wilful default. The defendant was not liable for the losses incurred. [1931] 1 Ch. 572

COMMENTARY

Maugham J. in an attempt to reconcile section 23 with section 30 of the *Trustee Act 1925*, interpreted the term "wilful default" in section 30 as meaning "a consciousness of negligence or

breach of duty, or recklessness in the performance of a duty"
(at 584). He relied on *Re City Equitable Fire Insurance Co.*
[1925] Ch. 407, a case involving the interpretation of a company's articles of association. There has been criticism of
Maugham J.'s interpretation. It has been argued that prior to
the 1925 Act, a trustee would be liable if he was negligent. As
the *Trustee Act 1925* is a consolidating Act, the presumption
is that the previous law has not been changed.

KEY PRINCIPLE: *Where section 30 of the Trustee Act 1925
is not applicable, the trustees' liability for the default or misconduct of an agent is based on the test of the ordinary man
of business as set out in Speight v. Gaunt.*

Re Lucking's Will Trusts 1968

Lucking was the sole trustee of a trust in which he was also one
of the beneficiaries. The trust consisted, *inter alia*, of a majority
shareholding in a private company. Lucking appointed Dewar,
a friend, as managing director to manage the company. Lucking signed blank cheques for Dewar's expenses. Lucking
became aware that Dewar was using company funds for his
own purposes but failed to do anything about it. Lucking
continued signing blank cheques for Dewar and although the
company's profits increased, its debts increased as well. Dewar
was dismissed from the company because of his debts to the
company and was subsequently adjudicated a bankrupt. The
plaintiff commenced an action against Lucking.

HELD: (Ch.D.) The facts of the present case did not fall
within the ambit of section 30 of the *Trustee Act 1925*. The
conduct of the trustee in this case was to be judged on the
basis of the ordinary prudent man of business as set out in
Speight v. Gaunt. Lucking was liable as he failed to supervise
Dewar, when he had known that the latter was dishonest.
[1968] 1 W.L.R. 866

COMMENTARY
Where the facts of the case does not fall within the ambit of
section 30 of the *Trustee Act 1925*, the liability of the trustee
for the default or misconduct of an agent is based on the

Speight v. Gaunt test. The *Vickery* test of wilful default would
not apply.

---

12. VARIATION OF TRUSTS

KEY PRINCIPLE: *Where the beneficiaries of a trust are
absolutely entitled, of full age, competent and of one mind,
they can terminate the trust.*

Saunders v. Vautier 1841

The testator bequeathed his East India stock to his trustees
upon trust to accumulate the interest and dividends until
Daniel Vautier reached the age of 25 years. Thereafter, the
stock, the accumulated interest and dividends were to be transferred to Daniel Vautier absolutely. Upon reaching the age of
21, Daniel Vautier applied for the transfer of the stock, the
accumulated interest and the dividends to him absolutely.

HELD: (Ch.) The trust fund should be transferred to him.
(1841) Beav. 115

COMMENTARY
[1] The case is authority for the proposition that where all the
beneficiaries are of full age, *sui juris* and absolutely entitled to
the trust fund, they can terminate the trust and direct the
trustees to transfer the trust fund to them even though this
may be against the testator's or settlor's intention.
[2] This is, however, an all-or-nothing process. The effect of
the rule is to terminate the existing trust: *Stephenson (Inspec-
tor of Taxes) v. Barclays Bank Trust Co. Ltd* [1975] 1 All E.R.
625.

Variation of Trusts at Common Law

KEY PRINCIPLE: *The court has an inherent jurisdiction to
vary the terms of a trust.*

Chapman v. Chapman 1954

The appellants who were trustees of various settlements,
applied for leave to execute a scheme of family arrangement
affecting the trust property or in the alternative, to release the

trust property from certain trusts under the settlements. The arrangement would have had certain tax advantages.

HELD: (HL) There was no inherent jurisdiction to sanction on behalf of infant beneficiaries and unborn persons, a rearrangement of the settlements for no other purpose than to secure a financial benefit. [1954] A.C. 429

COMMENTARY
Lord Simonds (at 445) stated that the court"s inherent jurisdiction to vary the terms of a trust was limited to:

- [a]   where property belonged beneficially to an infant, the court has a jurisdiction to change the nature of the property from real to personal and vice versa;
- [b]   where no provision was made for infant beneficiaries, the court assumed a jurisdiction to provide maintenance for the infant beneficiaries;
- [c]   to authorise a transaction which is not permitted by the trust by way of salvage;
- [d]   where the rights of infants and unborn beneficiaries are in dispute, the court may approve a compromise.

It should be noted that the category [c] would include cases of emergency where the trust has made not provision for. The *Variation of Trusts Act 1958* was subsequently introduced to complement the common law jurisdiction.

KEY PRINCIPLE: *The court's inherent jurisdiction to vary trusts includes allowing variation in cases of emergency for which the testator has made no provision.*

Re New 1901
The trustees of a trust held shares in a company which was undergoing reconstruction. The company proposed that all share holders in the existing company exchange their shares in return for shares and debentures in a new or reconstructed company. The trustees did not have the power to purchase or retain these types of shares.

HELD: (CA) As the evidence showed that the scheme would be of advantage to the beneficiaries of the trust, the court authorised the variation of the terms of the trust to allow the trustees to concur in the scheme and to hold the type of share to be issued. [1901] 2 Ch. 534

COMMENTARY
Before the court is prepared to exercise its inherent jurisdiction, there must be a genuine emergency or need. In *Re Tollemache* [1903] 1 Ch. 457, the court was not prepared to sanction a variation of the terms of the trust by allowing trust property to be mortgaged. This was because there was no emergency even though this may have been of benefit to the beneficiary.

KEY PRINCIPLE: *Where the testator has directed that income from the trust be accumulated but has made no provision for the maintenance or education of the beneficiaries, the court has an inherent jurisdiction to vary the trust to allow for the maintenance or education of the beneficiaries.*

Re Collins 1886

A testator directed that the income from his estate was to be accumulated for twenty-one years. The accumulated estate was to be given to his sister for life, then to her three sons and their male heirs in successive order.

HELD: (Ch.) The sister should be paid an annual sum out of the income of the estate for the maintenance and education of her sons. (1886) 32 Ch.D. 229

COMMENTARY
The inherent jurisdiction would only be used in cases where the statutory power of advancement or maintenance given to trustees under section 31 and 32 of the *Trustee Act 1925* has been excluded.

KEY PRINCIPLE: *The court has an inherent jurisdiction to vary the terms of a trust in order to reach a compromise in cases where a dispute has arisen.*

Chapman v. Chapman 1954

(See above).

HELD: (HL) The court did not have jurisdiction to approve the variation. In order for the court to avail itself of this jurisdiction, there had to be a genuine dispute for which the court could approve a compromise. [1954] A.C. 429

Mason v. Farbrother 1983

The applicants were trustees of the Co-operative Society members' Pension and Death Benefit Scheme. The Scheme was constituted by a trust deed executed in 1929 in which the trustees were given power to invest in the society itself and in authorised trustee investments. The trustees were uncertain whether the investment clause in the trust deed required them to invest all the funds either in the Society or in investments authorised by the *Trustee Investments Act 1961*. They also wished to have wider powers of investment. They applied to the court under its inherent jurisdiction to compromise disputed rights or alternatively, under section 57 of the *Trustee Act 1925*, to insert a wider investment clause.

HELD: (Ch.) The court did have the jurisdiction to approve a compromise of disputed rights and on the facts of the case there was a dispute as to the interpretation of the investment clause. However, it was doubtful whether the court had jurisdiction to substitute an entirely new investment clause for the existing investment clause in the trust deed. Therefore, the court would not sanction a variation of the terms of the trust under its inherent jurisdiction. [1983] 2 All E.R. 1078

COMMENTARY

In order for the court to exercise its inherent jurisdiction to approve a compromise of disputed rights, there must in fact be a dispute. Further, even if there is a dispute, there is a further requirement that the compromise must not be a total substitution of existing rights or powers, it must be a compromise.

Statutory Variation of Trusts

[i] Section 57 of the Trustee Act 1925

KEY PRINCIPLE: *The court has a jurisdiction to vary the terms of a trust where it is expedient for the administration or management of the trust.*

Re Downshire Settled Estates 1953

The plaintiff had a life interest under a settlement. He applied to the court to approve a scheme of arrangement which would have varied the beneficial interests. The application was made, *inter alia*, under section 57 of the *Trustee Act 1925* and/or section 64 of the *Settled Land Act 1925*.

HELD: (CA) The court did not have jurisdiction to approve a scheme of arrangement under section 57 of the *Trustee Act 1925* which would vary the beneficial interest. Its jurisdiction under that statutory provision was only with respect to the management or administration of the trust. The language of the section cannot be stretched to include any modification of the beneficial interests. [1953] 1 Ch. 218

Mason v. Farbrother 1983

(See above).

HELD: (Ch.) The court had jurisdiction under section 57 of the *Trustee Act 1925* to substitute wider investment powers. The court could use this jurisdiction where it considered that it would be expedient for the management and administration of trust property that the trustees should have wider powers of investment than that which was permitted under the trust deed. There were special circumstances in this case which entitled the court in exercising its jurisdiction under section 57 to substitute an investment clause which was wider than that allowed under the *Trustee Investments Act 1961*. [1983] 2 All E.R. 1078

COMMENTARY

The court's jurisdiction under section 57 of the *Trustee Act 1925* is restricted to cases where the variation of the terms of the trusts is in respect of the management or administration of the trust. Under this statutory provision, there is no power to vary the beneficial interests.

[ii] Variation under section 64 of the *Settled Land Act 1925*

KEY PRINCIPLE: *Under section 64 of the Settled Land Act 1925, the court can vary a settlement where this would be for the benefit of settled land or the persons entitled under the settlement.*

Re Downshire's Settled Estates 1953
(See above).

HELD: (CA) The scheme of arrangement was a transaction for the benefit of persons interested under the settlement which was within section 64 of the *Settled Land Act 1925*. Accordingly, the court would approve the scheme of arrangement. [1953] 1 Ch. 218

Hambro v. The Duke of Marlborough 1994
The tenant for life of a settlement created under the 1706 parliamentary settlement of Blenheim Palace, applied under section 64 of the *Settled Land Act 1925* to vary the beneficial interest of a beneficiary. This was done without the latter's consent.

HELD: (Ch.) The court had jurisdiction under section 64 to vary the beneficial interest without the beneficiary's consent where the variation is either for the benefit of settled land or all the beneficiaries under the settlement. [1994] Ch. 158

COMMENTARY
Section 64 of the *Settled Land Act 1925* gives the court jurisdiction to approve "any transaction" and was not restricted to variation of administrative and management matters in respect of the trust. It includes variation of the beneficial interest without the beneficiary's consent where the circumstances of the case justified it.

[iii] Section 53 of the Trustee Act 1925

KEY PRINCIPLE: *Section 53 of the Trustee Act 1925 gives the court jurisdiction to order the recovery and/or sale of trust property and apply the capital and income for the maintenance, education, or benefit of infant beneficiaries.*

Re Meux 1958
A life tenant of a trust applied to court under section 53 of the *Trustee Act 1925* to vary the trust in favour of his eldest son, who was an infant at the time.

HELD: (Ch.) The court had jurisdiction under section 53 to vary the trust as it was for the benefit of the infant. [1958] Ch. 154

[iv] Section 24 of the Matrimonial Causes Act 1973

KEY PRINCIPLE: *A husband's pension scheme is regarded as a postnuptial settlement in which the court has the power to vary the terms under section 24 of the Matrimonial Causes Act 1973.*

Brooks v. Brooks 1996

The husband's company pension scheme, of which the husband was the sole member, allowed him to make provision for his wife, after his death, upon his retirement. It further provided that the trustee could make a lump sum payment to a class of beneficiaries which included the wife. The wife presented a petition for divorce in 1989 and applied for financial provision. The husband claimed he was penniless and the question arose as to whether financial provision could be made from the pension fund.

HELD: (HL) The husband's pension scheme was a postnuptial settlement for the purposes of section 24 of the *Matrimonial Causes Act 1973*. The court, therefore, had power to vary the terms of the scheme, in so far as it constituted a settlement for the husband (the surplus belonging to the company), in favour of the wife. [1996] 1 A.C. 375

COMMENTARY
Their Lordships noted that in normal circumstances it would be reluctant to vary a pension scheme which would impact on other members of the scheme. In the present case, the court was prepared to vary the terms of the scheme as there was only one member. The scheme was varied by directing an immediate annuity and a deferred pension for the wife in priority to the husband.

[v] The Variation of Trusts Act 1958

KEY PRINCIPLE: *The Variation of Trusts Act 1958 does not allow for a complete resettlement of the trust.*

Re Towler's Settled Estates 1963

The trust fund of a settlement was held, subject to the applicant's life interest in half of the fund, on trust under which the applicant's daughter would be entitled to one quarter of the fund in possession on reaching the age of 21 and another quarter in remainder on the death of the applicant. The applicant's daughter was about to reach the age of 21 but had proven herself to be immature and irresponsible with money. The applicant applied under section 1 of the *Variation of Trusts Act 1958* for the court to approve the transfer the daughter's share to new trustees on protective trusts for the daughter for life, with remainder to her children or issue, or in default of children, to the other infant beneficiary interested under the settlement.

HELD: (Ch.) The court would not give its approval to the proposal because the jurisdiction conferred by the statute did not extend to a completely new resettlement. Even if did, the proposal went beyond what was necessary in the interests of the beneficiary. The court would, however, approve an alternative proposal deferring the payment of the capital for a further period but which would give her a protected life interest in the meantime. [1963] 3 All E.R. 759

Re Ball's Settlement Trusts 1968

The plaintiff had a life interest in a trust fund and a testamentary power to appoint, among others, to two of his sons. In default of appointment, the fund was to go to the two sons absolutely. He applied for the court's approval to an arrangement under the *Variation of Trusts Act 1958*, whereby his life interest, the power of appointment and the default provision, were to be replaced by the life interests for the two sons in equal shares. His son's children were to take the fund absolutely on the occurrence of certain events.

HELD: (Ch.) The court in the exercise of its jurisdiction under section 1 of the *Variation of Trusts Act 1958* could approve the variation on the behalf of all persons unknown or unascertained who may thereafter be beneficially interested. Although the new trusts were different from the original trust, the substratum of the old trust remained and the arrangement applied for could be described as a variation of the settlement. [1968] 1 W.L.R. 899

COMMENTARY

The dividing line between a resettlement and a variation giving rise to a new trust but with the substratum of the old trust remaining is a fine one. Although it is clear from *Re Steed's Will Trusts* [1959] 1 All E.R. 609 that the *Variation of Trusts*

Act 1958 had been drafted in a manner which gives the court the flexibility to consider any proposal put forward, the limitation is that it must be a variation and not a resettlement or substitution. The same approach was taken in *Re Holt's Settlement*, discussed below.

KEY PRINCIPLE: *The variation of trust under the Variation of Trusts Act 1958 must be of benefit to beneficiaries on whose behalf the court is being asked to give consent.*

Re Remnant's Settlement Trusts 1970

A trust in a will contained a forfeiture clause whereby the testator's grandchildren would forfeit their interest in the testator's estate if they were practicising Roman Catholics at the date of his daughter's death. The testator's two daughters applied to vary the trust including the removal of the forfeiture clause.

HELD: (Ch.) The court must be satisfied that the variation of the terms of the trust was of benefit to every person on whose behalf the court's consent was being sought. In deciding this, the court was bound to consider not merely their financial benefit but also benefit of any other kind and whether it was a fair and proper arrangement. Here, the proposed variation was fair and proper and was for the benefit of all the beneficiaries on whose behalf the court was asked to give consent. [1970] 1 Ch. 560

Re Weston's Settlements 1969

The plaintiff set up two trusts for the benefit of his children. He applied for a variation of the the trust to allow the trust to be moved to Jersey for tax purposes.

HELD: (CA) The court would not approve a variation of the trust to allow the trusts to be moved to Jersey. Lord Denning suggested that the court should not only consider monetary benefits. [1969] 1 Ch. 223

COMMENTARY

Under section 1 of the *Variation of Trusts Act 1958*, where the court is asked to consider whether the variation is one which would benefit the beneficiaries on whose behalf the court is being asked to give its consent, the benefit need not be financial benefit: *Re Holt's Settlements* [1968] 1 All E.R. 470. It can be a moral or social benefit: *Re C.L.* [1969] 1 Ch. 587.

KEY PRINCIPLE: *The variation of trust under the Variation of Trusts Act 1958 must be of benefit to the beneficiaries not merely as a class but also to them as individuals.*

Re Cohen's Settlement Trusts 1965

Under a settlement, the income from the trust fund was to be held on specified trusts until the death of all the settlor's sons. The fund was then to be divided between the settlor's grandchildren and their issue. The settlor's last surviving son applied to the court for approval under the *Variation of Trusts Act 1958* of a scheme which would replace the date of his death with a fixed date as the operative date when the settlor's grandchildren and their issue would take the capital.

HELD: (Ch.) The court would not approve the arrangement. Although the scheme would benefit the infant beneficiaries who were in existence between now and the fixed date, it was possible (although on the evidence not probable) that the settlor's son would survive the fixed date. This would result in beneficiaries born after the fixed date being deprived of their beneficial interest in the settlement. [1965] 1 W.L.R. 1229

COMMENTARY
Stamp J. was of the view that the court had to be satisfied that the proposed variation would be of benefit not only to the beneficiaries as a class but also be of benefit to each individual beneficiary on whose behalf consent is being sought under the 1958 Act.

KEY PRINCIPLE: *In exercising its discretion under the Variation of Trusts Act 1958, there is some uncertainty whether the court can take into account the testator's intention.*

Goulding v. James 1996

The testatrix made a will in 1992 in which she directed that her estate was to be given to her daughter, June, and June's husband, Kenneth, in equal shares. The will provided that if June or Kenneth predeceased the testatrix, their interest was to pass to their son, Marcus, when he reached 40. This will was revoked and a new will was drawn up in which June had a life interest in possession of the residuary estate subject to which Marcus was to take absolutely, provided he reached the age of 40. If Marcus died before that, then his children would take the estate absolutely. The testatrix died in December 1994. June and Marcus applied to court for a variation of the trust contained in the will under section 1(1)(c) of the *Variation of Trusts Act 1958*. The variation sought was for 45 per cent of the estate was to be held for June, 45 per cent for Marcus and the remaining 10 per cent for Marcus's children. Laddie J. declined to approve the arrangement as it was contrary to the testatrix's wishes.

HELD: (CA) In deciding whether or not approval should be granted under the 1958 Act, the court's only concern was that the arrangement must be "beneficial" to those for whom the court was asked to give consent. The purpose of the section was to enable a *Saunders v. Vautier* type of arrangement to occur when it would otherwise be precluded because there were beneficiaries who could not give their consent. The variation was approved. [1997] 2 All E.R. 239

COMMENTARY

Laddie J. at first instance, refused to approve the arrangement because it was contrary to the testatrix's intention. His view was that the court could take into account the testatrix's clear intention in deciding whether to exercise its discretion under the 1958 Act. However, there is nothing in the 1958 Act which imposes an obligation on the court to take into account the testatrix's intention. The Court of Appeal reversed Laddie J.'s decision on the basis that the court's only concern was that any variation was of benefit to those on behalf of whom the court was asked to approve the variation.

KEY PRINCIPLE: *In deciding whether to give consent under section 1 of the Variation of Trusts Act 1958, the court can take the type of risks which an adult beneficiary would be prepared to take on his own behalf.*

Re Holt's Settlement 1969

The plaintiff had a life interest under a settlement and, subject to her interest, was for her children upon attaining the age of 21 in equal shares. The plaintiff wished to surrender half the income in order to benefit her children but to have the trusts varied so that the children's interest would vest only when they attained the age of 30 and that income be accumulated at the trustees' discretion until the age of 25 or the earlier expiration of 21 years from the date of the court's order. The plaintiff applied for the court's approval to this arrangement on the behalf of persons unborn, who might become entitled under the trusts.

HELD: (Ch.) The court in reaching its decision, can take the type of risk which an adult beneficiary would take on their own behalf when considering whether the arrangement is of benefit to the beneficiaries. Here, as the proposed transaction was for the benefit of the beneficiaries on whose behalf the court was asked to give its consent, the arrangement would be approved. [1969] 1 Ch. 100

COMMENTARY

The court in reaching its decision under the 1958 Act, can attempt to balance the detriment and benefits to be derived from the proposed arrangement. If this entails a certain amount of risk, this is something which the court is entirely at liberty to do if it is the type of risk which an adult beneficiary would normally take. Contrast this with *Re Cohen's Settlement Trusts*, above.

KEY PRINCIPLE: *"Where property . . . is held on trusts . . . the court may if it thinks fit by order approve on behalf of . . .*

[b] *any person (whether ascertained or not) who may become entitled, directly or indirectly, to an interest under the trusts as being at a future date, or on the happening of a future event a person of any specified description or a member of any specified class of persons, so however that this paragraph shall not include*

any person who would be of that description, or a member of that class, as the case may be, if the said date had fallen or the said event had happened at the date of the application to the court". Section 1(1)(b) of the Variation of Trusts Act 1958.

Re Suffert's Settlement 1961

The applicant, who had a life interest under a protective trust in which her children were to take in remainder upon reaching the age of 21, applied to vary the terms of the trust. She had a general power of appointment in the event that she had no children. In default of appointment, the fund was to go to her statutory next of kin, which consisted of three adult cousins. One gave his consent to the application. The applicant was aged 61 and unmarried.

HELD: (Ch.) The variation sought could not bind the two adult cousins. The court did not have jurisdiction to approve the variation on their behalf under section 1 of the *Variation of Trusts Act 1958* because they fell under the proviso to section 1(1)(b). This was because they would be the statutory next of kin if the applicant had died at the time of the applicaiton. [1961] 1 Ch. 1

Knocker v. Youle 1986

The settlor's son and daughter applied to vary the terms of a trust. The trust directed that the income was to be paid to the daughter at 21, for life. She was given a general power of appointment to appoint those who would take after her in her will. In default of appointment, the income was to be paid to the settlor's wife for her life or until she remarried and subject to that, the trust fund was to be held on trust for the settllor's four sisters in equal shares and upon the death of any of the sisters, to her respective issue. The question was whether the court could give consent on behalf of the sisters' issue.

HELD: (Ch.) The court had no jurisdiction to approve the arrangement on behalf of the sisters' issue. Under section 1(1)(b) of the 1958 Act, a person who had an actual interest in the trust however remote, could not fall within the category of persons "who may become entitled". The sisters' issue had an interest under the trust, albeit a contingent one and since some of them also fell within the proviso to the subsection, the court could not approve the variation. [1986] 1 W.L.R. 934

COMMENTARY

In *Re Suffert's Settlement*, if the applicant had died at the date of the applicant, the two cousins would have become entitled under the settlement and was excluded by the proviso to section 1(1)(b) of the 1958 Act. In contrast, in *Re Moncrieff's Settlement Trusts* [1962] 1 W.L.R. 1344, where the facts were similar, except that the applicant had an adopted son who may have had an interest under settlement, the court was able to give its consent on behalf of the statutory next of kin. This was because they fell outside the proviso to section 1(1)(b) of the 1958 Act.

13. BREACH OF TRUST AND DEFENCES

Liability for Breach of Trust

KEY PRINCIPLE: *A trustee cannot avoid liability for breach of trust by merely leaving the decision-making to his co-trustees.*

Bahin v. Hughes 1886

One of the three trustees to a trust invested the money in an unauthorised security resulting in loss to the value of the fund. The beneficiary sued the trustees for breach of trust. The other two trustees sought to claim an indemnity from the trustee who wrongfully invested the money.

HELD: (CA) Where the management of the trust is left in hands of one of the trustees and that trustee commits a breach of trust, the trustees who have remained passive cannot claim an indemnity from the active trustee. [1886] 31 Ch. D. 390

COMMENTARY

Likewise, in *Townley v. Sherborne* (1634) Bridg. J. 35, the court held that a trustee was liable for the actions of a co-trustee by having left money in the latter's hands without enquiry.

KEY PRINCIPLE: *Where one trustee has made good the loss arising from a breach of trust, he can claim a contribution from the remaining trustees unless he is also a beneficiary.*

Chillingworth v. Chambers 1896

The plaintiff and defendant, who were trustees of a will, invested trust funds in unauthorised investments. The plaintiff subsequently became one of the beneficiaries under the will. Some of the unauthorised investments were made before he had become a beneficiary. The plaintiff and defendant were held jointly and severally liable for the loss which was made good out of the plaintiff's beneficial interest.

HELD: (CA) The plaintiff was not entitled to a contribution from the defendant in respect of any part of the loss. [1896] 1 Ch. 685

COMMENTARY

The general rule in cases where one trustee makes good the loss to the trust as a result of the trustees' breach of trust, he is entitled to claim a contribution from the other trustees. This is because the trustees are jointly and severally liable for the breach. However, where the trustee who has made good the loss is also a beneficiary, he is not entitled to a contribution from the others. This is because he is treated as having consented or instigated the breach in question.

KEY PRINCIPLE: *A trustee is not liable for the acts or default of an agent unless the trustee has been guilty of wilful default.*

Re Vickery 1931

(See Chap. 11).

HELD: (CA) The term wilful default in section 30 of the *Trustee Act 1925* meant a consciousness of negligence or breach of duty, or recklessness in the performance of a duty. [1931] 1 Ch. 472

COMMENTARY

Where a trustee delegates some of his functions to an agent, the trustee is not liable for the acts or defaults of the agent unless the trustee has been guilty of some form of recklessness rather than being merely negligent. As noted in Chapter 11, there is some doubt as to whether this decision is correct.

The Measure of Damages

KEY PRINCIPLE: *Where the trustees commit a breach of trust, they are liable to make good the loss.*

Bartlett v. Barclays Bank Trust Co. Ltd (No. 1) 1980

A trust owned 99.8 per cent of shares in a private company. The trust was managed by the trustees' department of the bank which later became the defendant trust corporation. In 1960 the defendant needed to raise money in order to pay death duties. It suggested that the private company should go public. The Board of Directors of the company wished to venture into property development. The defendant did not object and the company undertook two property development projects. One project failed whilst the other was a success. However, there was an overall loss. The beneficiaries commenced an action against the defendant.

HELD: (Ch.) In the case of the professional trustee, the duty of care imposed on such a trustee was higher than the standard of care of the ordinary prudent man of business. The defendant had failed in its duty to the trust and was therefore in breach of trust. Accordingly, the trustee was liable to make good the loss suffered by the trust. [1980] 1 Ch. 515

COMMENTARY

The measure of damages in cases of breach of trust by trustees is on the basis of restitution. The trustees must compensate the trust fully for any loss arising from the breach. In *Target Holdings Ltd v. Redferns* [1995] 3 All E.R. 785, Lord Browne-Wilkinson stated that (at 793) " . . . the basic rule is that a trustee in breach of trust must restore or pay to the trust estate either the assets which have been lost . . . or compensation for such loss . . . . [t]hus the common law rules of remoteness of damage and causation do not apply". However, Lord Browne-Wilkinson went onto say that there must be some causal connection between the breach of trust and the loss caused to the estate.

KEY PRINCIPLE: *The principles used in assessing compensation for loss resulting from a breach of trust depends on the* *nature of the fiduciary duty which had been breached and whether the trust is a traditional trust or a commercial arrangement.*

Target Holdings Ltd v. Redferns (A Firm) 1995

The defendant firm of solicitors acted for the plaintiff mortgagee and the mortgagor. The plaintiff alleged that it was the victim of a mortgage fraud. The mortgagor agreed to purchase a property for £775,000 but it was negligently valued by the second defendant at £2m. The plaintiff agreed to grant a loan of £1,525,000 secured on the property. The defendant paid over the loan monies, which it held on trust for the mortgagee, prior to the completion of the purchase or the charge. The mortgagor subsequently became insolvent and the property was sold by the plaintiff for £500,000. The plaintiff sued the first defendant, *inter alia*, for breach of trust. The defendant argued that there had only been a technical breach and the plaintiff suffered no loss because they had the mortgage to which they were entitled. The plaintiff applied for summary judgment.

HELD: (HL) A trustee who committed a breach of trust was not liable to compensate a beneficiary for loss suffered if the loss would still have occured irregardless of the breach. In the present case, where there was a bare trust arising from a conveyancing transaction, once the transaction was completed, the solicitor's client account could not be reconstituted as a trust fund. Notwithstanding the breach of trust by the defendant, the plaintiff had obtained what they would have obtained if no breach occurred, namely, a valid enforceable mortgage. The plaintiff had therefore suffered no compensatable loss. The defendant was entitled to leave to defend the action. [1995] 3 All E.R. 785

COMMENTARY
The decision makes a clear distinction between the traditional type trust and the trust arising out of a commercial transaction. In the latter, the basis of compensation for breach of trust is by analogy to common law damages— that the plaintiff is to be put in the position he would be in if the breach had not occurred. In the case itself, the plaintiff would have suffered the loss notwithstanding the breach and

therefore the defendant was not liable to pay the plaintiff anything more than nominal damages. However, that would be dependent on the evidence in the trial itself. In the case of a breach of trust in the traditional type trust, the obligation on the trustees is to account for, and restore to, the trust fund that which has been lost. Lord Browne Wilkinson's dictum in *Bartlett v. Barclays Bank Trust Co Ltd (No. 1)* (above), applies here.

KEY PRINCIPLE: *If the trustees make an unauthorised investment, the trustees will be liable to make good the loss even though the sale was ordered by the court and there was a possibility that the investment would not have resulted in a loss if it had been retained.*

Knott v. Cottee 1852

An executor invested part of the estate in Exchequer Bills in 1846. The court ordered the sale of the investment. The investment was sold that same year but at a loss. In 1848, the court declared that the investment was improper but the price of the Bills had risen by then.

HELD: (Ch.) The executor was liable for the loss arising from the sale because he had made an improper investment, even though the sale was ordered by the court and the investment would not have resulted in a loss if it had been retained.(1852) 16 Beav. 77.

KEY PRINCIPLE: *Where the trustees retain investments improperly, they will be liable for the difference in value between the value when it should have been sold and its present value.*

Fry v. Fry 1859

A testator directed his executors and trustees to sell his freehold inn as soon as convenient after his death. The testator died in 1834. The trustees received an offer of £900 for the inn in 1836 but they refused to sell. The value of the inn subsequently depreciated in value. The inn remained unsold in 1859 by which time both the trustees had died.

HELD: (Ch.) The trustees' estates were liable for the difference in value between the £900 and the present value of the inn. (1859) 27 Beav. 144

COMMENTARY
The principle is clearly one of restitution to the trust.

KEY PRINCIPLE: *Where the trustees improperly sell an authorised investment they must replace it or pay the difference between the sale price and the cost of repurchasing the investment.*

Phillipson v. Gatty 1848

Trustees of a settlement who had the power to invest trust funds in Government stock or real security, sold the stock. The proceeds of sale were improperly invested in a mortgage.

HELD: The whole transaction including the sale of the stock must be taken as one unjustifiable transaction and therefore the trustees had to replace the stock. (1848) 7 Hare. 516

COMMENTARY
In *Re Bell's Indenture* [1980] 1 W.L.R. 1217, the court decided that the loss to the trust should be assessed at the date of the judgment. Thus, where an asset has to be repurchased, this will be as at the date of the judgment and not the date of the breach or the date when the action was commenced.

KEY PRINCIPLE: *Where the trustees make a loss on one unauthorised transaction but make a profit on another unauthorised transaction, they cannot set off the profit against the loss, unless they are part of the same transaction.*

Bartlett v. Barclays Bank Trust Co. Ltd (No. 1) 1980

(See above).

HELD: (Ch.) That the defendant trustee was allowed to set off the profit from one project against the loss from the other project as it could be said to have stemmed from the same policy. [1980] 1 Ch. 515

COMMENTARY

On the facts of that particular case, the set off was allowed. In *Dimes v. Scott* (1828) 4 Russ. 195, it was decided that trustees would not be entitled to set off the loss made from a breach of trust against the profit arising from another breach of trust. The trust is entitled to keep the profit and be fully compensated for the loss. In *Re Bell's Indenture* (above), the court noted that if the tax liability of the trust has been reduced as a result of a breach of trust, the trustee will not be entitled to the benefit from this. The trustee cannot therefore, set off this reduction in tax against his liability to compensate the trust.

KEY PRINCIPLE: *The court has an inherent jurisdiction to award interest in appropriate cases.*

Wallersteiner v. Moir (No. 2) 1975

The defendant, a minority shareholder in a company, made allegations against the plaintiff, who was one of the directors. The defendant was sued for libel. The defendant counterclaimed seeking declarations that the plaintiff had been guilty of fraud, misfeasance and breach of trust. The plaintiff did not defend the counterclaim and judgment was given for the defendant together with interest. The plaintiff appealed claiming that the court did not have jurisdiction to award interest.

HELD: (CA) The court had an inherent jurisdiction to award interest where a fiduciary had benefitted from his position. The rate of interest would be fixed at 1 per cent above the minimum bank lending rate. [1975] Q.B. 373

COMMENTARY

The court has an inherent jurisdiction to award interest in cases where there has been a breach of trust. However, it is clear that this is not to punish the trustee but to ensure that the trustee has not benefitted from the breach of trust. In some cases, a higher rate of interest may be imposed where the trustee has himself received a higher rate (*Re Emmet's Estate* (1881) 17 Ch. D. 142), where he ought to have received a higher rate of interest (*Jones v. Foxall* (1852) 21 L.J. Ch. 725), or where he is presumed to have received a commercial rate (*O'Sullivan v. Management Agency and Music Ltd* [1984] 3 W.L.R. 448).

Defences to an Action for Breach of Trust

[a] Laches and Limitation Act 1980

KEY PRINCIPLE: *The limitation period does not apply where the cause of action relates to any fraud or fraudulent breach of trust to which the trustee was a party or privy to: Section 21 (1)(a) of the Limitation Act 1980.*

Thorne v. Heard 1895

The respondent mortgagees sold the mortgaged property under their power of sale in 1878. They used the mortgagor's solicitor to conduct the sale. The solicitor received the proceeds of sale and after payment of the respondents' mortgage kept the balance of the proceeds without paying off the second mortgage. The solicitor continued to pay interest on the second mortgage as if the mortgage was still subsisting. The second mortgagee discovered the fraud in 1892 and brought an action against the respondents for an account and payment of money due.

HELD: (HL) The second mortgagee's action was barred by the Statute of Limitations. The respondents were not party or privy to the fraud which was perpetrated by the solicitor, who was independent of the respondents, nor were the proceeds of sale still in their hands. [1895] A.C. 495

COMMENTARY

The normal limitation period for an action for breach of trust or for the recovery of trust property (apart from infringement of the self dealing rule), must be commenced within six years from the date the cause of action accrued: section 21(3) of the *Limitation Act 1980.* Where fraud is involved, the limitation period does not apply. However, the fraud must be the fraud of or in some way imputable to the person who relies on the Limitation Act and not a third party.

KEY PRINCIPLE: *" . . . [f]or the purposes of this subsection, the right of action shall not be treated as having accrued to any beneficiary entitled to a future interest in the trust property* *until the interest fell into possession." Section 21(3) of the Limitation Act 1980.*

Re Pauling's Settlement Trusts 1964
(See Chap. 11).
The trustees pleaded, *inter alia*, that the limitation period ran from the time the improper advances were made and therefore the beneficiaries were time barred from suing the trustees.

HELD: (CA) The beneficiaries had a future interest and therefore the time limit did not start to run until they received their entitlement. The time limit did not run from when the advances were made. [1964] Ch. 303

COMMENTARY
The proviso to section 21(3) of the *Limitation Act 1980* applied. The limitation period only began to run when they received their full shares under the trust and not before. Therefore, the beneficiaries' action against the trustees was not time barred.

KEY PRINCIPLE: *Where the Limitation Act 1980 does not apply, the defendant may rely on the defence of laches.*

Nelson v. Rye 1996
The plaintiff, who was a musician, retained the defendant to act as his manager between 1980 and 1990. The defendant failed to account to the plaintiff on a regular. In 1990 the plaintiff terminated the agreement and commenced an action against the defendant. The defendant argued that the claim for an account for the period prior to 1985 was time barred under the *Limitation Act 1980* and that the equitable defence of laches and acquiescence applied. The plaintiff replied that as his claim was for breach of fiduciary duty or breach of trust, the Limitation Act did not apply.

HELD: (Ch) The defendant was under a fiduciary duty to the plaintiff to account regularly. He had breached this duty and received monies belonging to the plaintiff, which was trust property. Accordingly, the *Limitation Act 1980* did not apply. In deciding whether the equitable doctrine of laches and acquiescence applied, the court would take into account the circumstances of the case which would include the reason and period of delay and the extent of the prejudice to the defendant as a result of the delay. In the circumstances of the case, there had been an unreasonable delay because the plaintiff had been reluctant to involve himself in financial matters. Consequently, it would be unfair and unjust to allow the plaintiff's claim pre-1985. [1996] 2 All E.R. 186

COMMENTARY

The doctrine of laches applies in those cases where the *Limitation Act 1980* does not. This would include cases where there is an allegation that the trustee has been party to or privy to a fraud, or where the claim is against trustees for property or proceeds of sale improperly retained by them or claims against trustees for the infringement of the self dealing rule. In such cases, depending on the circumstances of the case, the claim may be barred where there has been an unreasonable long period of delay causing prejudice to the defendant. This decision has been followed recently in *Kershaw v. Whelan (No 2), The Times*, February 10, 1997.

[b] Release, consent and acquiescence

KEY PRINCIPLE: *Where the beneficiaries, upon discovering a breach of trust, release or acquiesce to the breach, they cannot thereafter claim against the trustee for that breach of trust.*

Re Pauling's Settlement Trusts 1964

(See Chap. 11).
One of the issues was whether the plaintiff beneficiaries had acquiesced to the breach of trust.

HELD: (CA) The plaintiffs could not be said to have acquiesced to the breach of trust unless they knew or ought to have known what their rights were. Here, the plaintiffs were not aware of their rights until they were subsequently advised that the advances may have been improper. Accordingly, the plaintiffs were not debarred from their action by reason of acquiescence. [1964] 1 Ch. 303

COMMENTARY

Generally, in order for the trustees to be able to establish acquiescence on the part of the beneficiaries, they need to show that the beneficiaries by their conduct impliedly agreed not to enforce their strict legal rights. It should be noted that the beneficiaries could have waived their rights against the trustees.

KEY PRINCIPLE: *Where a beneficiary consents to a breach of trust, he is not entitled to claim compensation from the trustees to the extent of his beneficial interest.*

Fletcher v. Collis 1905

Property was settled on a husband for life, thereafter to the wife for life and the remainder to the children. In 1885, the whole of the trust property was sold at the wife's request with the husband's consent. The money was handed over to the wife who spent it. The husband was then adjudicated a bankrupt. The trustee replaced the trust property after an action against him had been commenced by the beneficiaries. The trustee died after this had been done but there was a surplus which represented the income. The trustee's personal representative claimed this on the basis that this was partial indemnity from the husband. The husband's trustee in bankruptcy disputed this.

HELD: (CA) As the husband had consented to the breach of trust, he could not require the trustee to make good his loss of income resulting from the breach. Accordingly, the trustee in bankruptcy had no claim to the surplus.[1905] 2 Ch. 24

[c] Impounding the beneficiary's interest

KEY PRINCIPLE: *Under section 62 of the Trustee Act 1925, where a trustee commits a breach of trust at the instigation, request or consent of a beneficiary, the court may impound the beneficiary's interest.*

Re Somerset 1894

The tenant for life of a marriage settlement requested the trustees to invest part of the trust funds in a mortgage of a particular property. The trustees followed his request but lent too much on the mortgage. The beneficiaries commenced an action against the trustees for the resulting loss.

HELD: (CA) Although the tenant for life had requested that the investment be made, he did not intend to be a party to any breach of trust or to an investment in the mortgage without enquiry. He left it to the trustees to determine whether the investment was a proper investment. Accordingly, the tenant for life's interest would not be impounded. [1894] 1 Ch. 231

COMMENTARY
The case concerned the predecessor to section 62 of the *Trustee Act 1925*. The rule is that in order for the beneficiary's interest to be impounded, it was necessary to show not only that the beneficiary's request resulted in the breach of trust but must also have been aware that the action would result in such a breach.

[d] Section 61 of the Trustee Act 1925

KEY PRINCIPLE: *Under section 61 of the Trustee Act 1925, the court may relieve a trustee either wholly or partly, where he is personally liable for a breach of trust, if he has acted honestly and reasonably and ought fairly to be excused.*

Perrins v. Bellamy 1899
The trustees of a settlement committed a breach of trust in reliance upon the erroneous advice of their solicitor. The plaintiff commenced an action for breach of trust.

HELD: (CA) Although there was a breach of trust, the trustees had acted both honestly and reasonably and therefore the trustees ought to be relieved from personal liability. [1899] 1 Ch. 797

National Trustees Co. of Australasia Ltd v. General Finance Co. of Australasia Ltd 1905
The appellant trustees wrongly paid over two-thirds of the trust fund to the beneficiaries in reliance upon the erroneous advice of their solicitor. The issue arose as to whether the trustees should be relieved from liability.

HELD: (PC) A trustee is not entitled to be relieved from liability merely by showing that he acted honestly and reasonably. The trustee must satisfy the court that in all the circumstances of the case, he ought fairly to be excused. Here, the trustee had acted honestly and reasonably but had failed to show why it ought fairly to be excused from liability. [1905] A.C. 373

COMMENTARY
Both cases concerned the equivalent of section 61 of the *Trustee Act 1925*. In *Perrins v. Bellamy*, the court suggested that the trustees ought to be excused if they had shown that they acted honestly and reasonably without showing that the trustees ought fairly to be excused. However, in *National Trustees Co. of Australia Ltd v. General Finance Co of Australasia Ltd.* the Privy Council insisted that there must be further evidence to show that in the circumstances of the case, the trustees ought fairly to be excused. It may have been relevant that the trustee in the latter case was a professional trustee and, therefore, a higher standard of care was imposed. This is reinforced by *Re Pauling's Settlement Trusts* [1964] Ch. 303, below. In *Bartlett v. Barclays Bank Trust Co. Ltd* (above), the court refused to excuse a trustee's breach of trust under section 61 of the *Trustee Act 1925* because, although the trustee had acted honestly, it had not acted reasonably.

KEY PRINCIPLE: *Where a trustee committed a breach of trust in circumstances where there was a conflict of duty and interest, the court is reluctant to grant the trustee relief under section 61 of the Trustee Act 1925.*

Re Pauling's Settlement Trusts 1946
(See Chap. 11).

HELD: (CA) Where a bank acted as a paid trustee and had placed itself in a position where its interest as a banker was in conflict with its duty as a trustee, the court would be reluctant to grant it relief under section 61 of the *Trustee Act 1925*. [1964] 1 Ch. 303

COMMENTARY
It should be noted that the court did not decide that relief was unobtainable but merely that it would be slow to grant a trustee in the position of the Bank, relief under section 61. That would suggest that if there were exceptional circumstances, the court may be prepared to grant such relief but such occasions would undoubtedly be rare.

KEY PRINCIPLE: *The court may relieve the trustee from liability in whole or in part under section 61 of the Trustee Act 1925.*

Re Kay 1897

The testator's estate consisted of assets worth £22,000. It was initially thought that there were debts of about £100. The executor paid out a legacy to the widow and provided moneys for the maintenance and education of the children. A creditor subsequently claimed £26,000 from the estate.

HELD: (Ch) The executor had acted reasonably and honestly. They would be relieved from liability up until the time the creditor's claim was received. Thereafter, they were liable for the payments which they made. [1897] 2 Ch. 518

COMMENTARY

It is clear from the statutory provision that relief can be given either wholly or in part. This case is an example where it was appropriate to grant partial relief.

---

14. PROPRIETARY REMEDIES—TRACING

Tracing at Common Law

KEY PRINCIPLE: *Where the property in the asset has not passed, the claimant can trace the asset into the hands of the party holding the property.*

Taylor v. Plumer 1815

The defendant gave money to his stockbroker for the purchase of exchequer bonds. However, the stockbroker bought American investments and bullion. The defendant pursued the stockbroker and was able to seize the investments. The investments were subsequently sold. The stockbroker was declared bankrupt and his assignees in bankruptcy sought an order that the proceeds of sale belonged to them.

HELD: The defendant was entitled to retain the proceeds of sale as the property in them had not passed and was identifiable. (1815) 2 Rose. 415

COMMENTARY

Tracing at common law is available where the property in the asset has not passed. However, such a remedy is not available to a beneficiary under a trust or a claim in equity.

KEY PRINCIPLE: *The property must be identifiable in order for tracing to be available at common law.*

Banque Belge pour L'Etranger v. Hambrouck 1921

The first defendant fraudulently obtained cheques from his employer drawn on the plaintiff bank. These amounted to about £6,000 and were paid into his bank account. The first defendant then drew cheques on his account and paid them to another defendant, a Ms Spanoghe, with whom he was living. She paid these cheques into her bank account. When the fraud was discovered there was £315 in her bank account. The plaintiff bank sought a declaration that the money was their property and an order that it should be paid to them.

HELD: (CA) The money was capable of being traced. The plaintiff bank was therefore entitled to the declaration and the order sought. [1921] 1 K.B. 321

COMMENTARY

[1] In this case, tracing at common law was available because no other moneys were paid into Ms Spanoghe's bank account apart from the proceeds of the fraud. The money was therefore identifiable. Once the monies has been mixed with other property, tracing at common law is not available.

[2] Further, the property in the money had not passed to Ms Spanoghe as she had not given any consideration for it.

KEY PRINCIPLE: *Tracing at common law is lost where the moneys have been mixed in intervening accounts in the bank clearing system.*

Agip (Africa) Ltd v. Jackson 1992
(See Chap. 8).
The plaintiff, *inter alia*, sought to recover the money on the basis of money had and received.

HELD: (CA) The common law remedy of tracing was not available. The difficulty was in identifying the origin of money. This could not be done without tracing the money through the New York clearing system where it would have been mixed with other funds. It could not be established at common law that the money with which the Lloyds Bank had been paid was the money from the Tunis Bank. [1991] Ch. 547

COMMENTARY
[1] The Court of Appeal stated that in determining whether common law tracing was available as a remedy, it did not matter that the money had been transmitted by telegraphic transfer. At first instance, Millet J.'s view was that where the money had been transmitted via telegraphic transfer between banks it was impossible to trace the money at common law. The issue is not method of payment, but at common law, it is the question of whether it is possible to follow the physical asset from one recipient to another. Where the money has been mixed with other moneys, common law tracing is not available.
[2] A similar conclusion was reached in *Bank Tejarat v. Hong Kong & Shanghai Banking Corportion (CI) Ltd* [1995] 1 Lloyds L.R. 239.

KEY PRINCIPLE: *Any profit arising from the use of the money or asset which is subject to tracing has to be paid over.*

Trustee of the property of FC Jones and Sons (a firm) v. Jones 1996
The partners of the firm of FC Jones and Sons were adjudicated bankrupt. Before this, the defendant who was the wife of one of the partners paid money to a firm of commodity brokers to invest. She subsequently received £50,760 from the brokers. The Official Receiver claimed to be entitled to this money. The defendant argued that although the original sum paid to the brokers belonged to the Receiver, she was entitled to keep the profits from the investments.

HELD: (CA) The defendant's contention was rejected. The Official Receiver's claim to trace the funds was at common law and was entitled to both the original sum and the profits generated by it. *The Times*, May 13, 1996.

COMMENTARY
This is a recent example of tracing at common law. Tracing in equity did not apply because the defendant had not received the money as a fiduciary.

Tracing in Equity

[a] A fiduciary relationship must be present.

KEY PRINCIPLE: *There must be a fiduciary relationship between the parties in order for the remedy of tracing to be available in equity.*

Re Hallett's Estate 1880
A solicitor held bonds for his own settlement as well as for a client. He sold the bonds without consent and paid the proceeds of sale into his bank account. Money was deposited and drawn out from the account by the solicitor for his own use. The solicitor then died.

HELD: (CA) The right to trace in equity was available in cases where there was a fiduciary relationship between the parties and was not limited to the trustee-beneficiary relationship. The client and the beneficiaries of the settlement were therefore entitled to trace in equity as a fiduciary relationship existed between them. (1880) 13 Ch. D. 696

Sinclair v. Brougham 1914
A building society carried on an *ultra vires* banking business. It was ordered to be wound up and the question arose as to the priority between the shareholders, creditors and customers who had deposited money. It was accepted that the creditors were entitled to be paid first. The issue was whether the shareholders had priority over the customers.

HELD: (HL) The customers who deposited money in the bank were not entitled to recover the money on the basis of money had and received. However, they were entitled to trace the funds into the hands of the building society as there was a fiduciary relationship between the building society and the customers but they ranked in *pari passu* with the shareholders. [1914] A.C. 398

COMMENTARY
In *AGIP (Africa) Ltd v. Jackson* [1990] 1 Ch. 265, Millet J., at first instance, noted that the requirement of a fiduciary relationship before tracing was available in equity had been widely condemned and was dependent on authority rather than principle. He was of the view that this principle should be reconsidered but did not think it was appropriate to do so at first instance. Notwithstanding the criticisms, it would seem that the position is now well settled, in that, before tracing in equity is available, the existence of a fiduciary relationship is a necessary prerequisite. The requirement of a fiduciary relationship has been accepted by the *House of Lords in West-deutsche Landesbank Girozentrale v. Islington Borough Council* [1996] A.C. 669.

KEY PRINCIPLE: *The fiduciary relationship necessary for tracing to be available in equity can sometimes arise out of the circumstances of the case.*

Chase Manhattan Bank NA v. Israel-British Bank (London) Ltd 1981

The plaintiff mistakenly paid a sum of US $2m to a bank which in turn paid it to the defendant. The defendant subsequently went into liquidation. The plaintiff sought to trace and recover in equity the sum erroneously paid.

HELD: (Ch.) Where money was erroneously paid under a mistake of fact, the payer retained an equitable interest in the money. The payee was subject to a fiduciary duty to respect the proprietary interest of the payer. Accordingly, the plaintiff was entitled to trace the money. [1981] 1 Ch. 105.

Re Goldcorp Exchange Ltd (in receivership) 1995

A company which dealt in gold and other precious metals sold unascertained bullion to the first respondents on a "non-allocated basis" for future delivery. The company stored and insured the bullion. The respondents had the right to call for delivery of their portion within seven days. The company encountered financial difficulties and the Bank of New Zealand appointed receivers under the terms of a debenture issued by the company. The receivers applied for directions on the disposal of the bullion. At first instance, the High Court of New Zealand rejected the first respondents' claims but the Court of Appeal allowed their claim on different grounds.

HELD: (PC)

- [i] The first respondents had no title in law or in equity to any of the bullion since they had contracted to purchase unascertained goods. No title could pass until the bullion had become ascertained goods.
- [ii] The moneys which had been paid by the first respondent to the company were not impressed with a trust thereby entitling them to trace into the company's assets. Neither was the company a fiduciary with respect to the monies as these were paid by the respondents in performance of the contract. [1995] 1 A.C. 74

COMMENTARY

[1] In *Chase Manhattan Bank NA v. Israel-British Bank (London) Ltd*, Goulding J. (at 119) emphasised that the fund to be traced need not have been the subject of fiduciary obligations. It was enough that the payment of the money into the wrong hands gave rise to a fiduciary relationship. In reaching this conclusion, he relied on *Sinclair v. Broughman*, above, where there was no intention between the directors of the building society and the customers to create a fiduciary relationship but that nonetheless, a fiduciary relationship arose out of the payment of the money to the Building Society. He also stressed that there was no need for the fiduciary relationship to arise from a consensual transaction. The fiduciary relationship can also arise from the terms of a contract between the parties. See: *Aluminium Industrie Vaasen BV v. Romalpa Aluminium Ltd* [1976] 1 W.L.R. 676.

[2] The decision in *Chase Manhattan* was applied by the New Zealand Court of Appeal in *Re Goldcorp Exchange* (at that stage the case was known as *Liggett v. Kensington* [1993] 1 N.Z.L.R. 257) where it was held that a fiduciary relationship existed between the company and the respondents because the respondents acquired a proprietary interest in the bullion. However, the Privy Council was of the view that no fiduciary

relationship existed between the company and the respondents. Lord Mustill refused to express any view on whether *Chase Manhattan* had been decided correctly. However, doubt has been cast in the correctness of *Chase Manhattan* by the House of Lords in *Westdeutsche Landesbank Girozentrale v. Islington Borough Council* [1996] A.C. 669.

[3] The necessary fiduciary relationship can be established where the person against whom the claim is being brought has been held to be a constructive trustee: *Att.-Gen. of Hong Kong v. Reid* [1993] A.C. 713 (see Chap. 8).

[b] Third parties

KEY PRINCIPLE: *Tracing in equity is available against volunteers.*

Re Diplock 1948

The testator left his residuary estate to be applied for such charitable or benevolent objects as his executors should so decide. The executors distributed the estate amongst a number of charities. It was subsequently declared that the gift was invalid as it was not wholly and exclusively charitable. An action was commenced by the next of kin, *inter alia*, to trace the money into the hands of the charities who were volunteers.

HELD: (CA) The claim by the next of kin to trace the money into the charities' hands would succeed. This was notwithstanding that the charities had mixed the monies from the estate with their own moneys. However, the charities were entitled to assert their own claim to the mixed funds so that the charities and the claimant would share *pari passu* in the mixed fund. Where the trust moneys have not been mixed with the charities' own funds, the charities would hold the moneys on trust for the true owner. Further, the application of the remedy must not result in injustice. [1948] 1 Ch. 465

COMMENTARY
[1] The next of kin succeeded in their claim to trace against the charities by establishing that there was a fiduciary relationship between the parties. The court's view was that it would not be inequitable to trace into the hands of innocent volunteers in this case.

[2] The court also stated that tracing would not succeed

against a party who has received the trust moneys (or trust property) for value without notice of the claimant's equitable interest in it. The claimant's equitable interest to that extent would be extinguished.

[3] The claimant also succeeded in a claim *in personam* on the basis that there was an equity to recover from a recipient who was wrongly or over paid and such a remedy was available to an unpaid or underpaid creditor, legatee or next of kin.

[c] The property must be in a traceable form.

KEY PRINCIPLE: *The remedy of tracing in equity is not available where the money has been used to pay off loans or the asset has been dissipated.*

Re Diplock 1948
(See above).
One of the issues which arose was whether it was possible to trace in cases where the money had been used to pay off loans or where the moneys have been used to improve properties.

HELD: (CA) Where the trust money had been used to pay off loans, the money is regarded as having been lost and therefore it is not possible to use the remedy with regard to this sum of money. Further, where the charities had expended money on the alteration or improvements of their assets, or by erecting buildings on the land, the trust money could not be disentangled from the asset or land and therefore an application of the remedy of tracing would result in injustice. [1948] Ch. 465

Boscawen v. Bajwa 1995
The solicitors for the purchaser of the defendant's property also acted for the Abbey National who was providing the loan for the purchase of the property. A sum of £140,000 was transferred to the solicitors to be used to complete the purchase and until then it was to be held for the Abbey National. The solicitors paid £137,405 to the defendant's solicitors to hold for the former's order until completion. Further, a cheque for the balance of £2,595 which was issued by the purchaser's solicitors was dishonoured. Just prior to that, the defendant's solicitors had paid £140,000 to the defendant's mortgagee to discharge the mortgage. However, the sale fell through and the

plaintiff, who was a creditor of the defendant, obtained a charging order absolute over the property. The property was later sold and the net proceeds of sale was paid into court. The issue arose as to who had a better claim to the money.

HELD: (CA) The Abbey National was entitled to the proceeds of sale as it had priority over the plaintiff. The Abbey National was entitled to be subrogated to the defendant's mortgagee legal charge as the money provided by it could be traced into the payment to the defendant's mortgagee. [1995] 4 All E.R. 853

COMMENTARY
The decision in *Re Diplock* has been followed by Scottish courts in *Style Financial Services Ltd v. Bank of Scotland, The Times,* May 23, 1995. In *Boscawan v. Bajwa,* the court distinguished *Re Diplock.* Millet L.J.'s view was that the favourable treatment given to innocent volunteers who mixed trust monies with his own in *Re Diplock* could not be applied to the facts of the present case. The parties were not wholly innocent volunteers although their conduct did fall short of dishonesty. Therefore, unlike *Re Diplock,* in *Boscawen v. Bajwa,* although the money was used to pay off what is essentially a loan, it could not be regarded as having been totally dissipated and accordingly the Abbey National could be subrogated to the position of the defendant's mortgagee and claim the proceeds of sale.

KEY PRINCIPLE: *The remedy of tracing in equity cannot be used to trace into an overdrawn bank account.*

Bishopsgate Investment Management Ltd (in liquidation) v. Homan 1994
The plaintiff was the trustee of some pension schemes out of which moneys had been improperly withdrawn. These moneys were paid into the bank account of one of the Maxwell companies, which became insolvent. The bank account subsequently became overdrawn. The liquidators of the plaintiff company sought to trace into this bank account.

HELD: (CA) The remedy of tracing in equity did not extend to tracing through an overdrawn bank account whether it had been overdrawn at the time the money was paid in or subsequently. [1994] 3 W.L.R. 1270

COMMENTARY
Where the money in question has been paid into an overdrawn account, the money is treated as having been lost and therefore tracing cannot be used. This is in line with earlier decisions such as *Re Diplock* (see above).

KEY PRINCIPLE: *Where the trustee mixes the funds of two trusts or an innocent volunteer mixes trust funds with his own moneys, the rule in Clayton's case may be applied where it does not result in injustice.*

Clayton's Case 1816

D was the senior partner of a firm of bankers where C was a client. After D's death C continued business with the firm until it went bankrupt. C made a claim against D's estate for the amount due to him from the firm at the date of D's death. Although the amounts paid by the firm to C after D's death was enough to pay the amount outstanding at D's death, C argued that these related to the amounts subsequently paid in by him to the account thereby leaving the original amount outstanding.

HELD: A presumption that payments in were appropriated to the debts in the order they were incurred would apply in the case of a current account such as bank account. This presumption would not arise where there was an express declaration to the contrary at the time of payment. Since this was absent in this case, the presumption applied and therefore debts outstanding at the date of D's death had been fully discharged. (1816) 1 Mer. 572

Barlow Clowes International Ltd (in liquidation) v. Vaughan 1992

The plaintiff investment company went into liquidation and the issue arose as to whether the investors were entitled to trace into the remaining funds of the company under the rule in *Clayton's* case.

HELD: (CA) The rule in *Clayton's* case was a convenient method of determining competing claims where several beneficiaries' money had been mixed together in one account. Where injustice would result from its application or be impractical, the rule will not be applied. On the facts of the case, if the rule was to be applied, injustice would result. In the circumstances of the case, there was an alternative method of distribution. It was therefore appropriate to order the investors to share the funds of the company on a *pari passu* basis in proportion to the amounts due to them. [1992] 4 All E.R. 22

COMMENTARY

The rule in *Clayton's* case is often referred to as the "first in first out" rule, *i.e.* that the money paid in first is deemed to have been withdrawn first. This rule only applies in cases where the funds of two trusts are mixed together or where an innocent volunteer mixes his own moneys with trust funds. It does not apply where trust moneys are mixed with the trustee's own funds. Further, as noted in *Barlow Clowes International Ltd (in liquidation) v. Vaughan*, this is merely a rule of convenience and where it would be impractical or injustice would result from its application, the court need not apply it.

KEY PRINCIPLE: *Where a trustee mixes trust funds with his own moneys, the trustee is presumed to have used his money first before the trust funds are used.*

Re Hallett's Estate 1880

(See above).

HELD: (CA) The trustee or fiduciary is deemed to have used his own moneys first before using trust moneys where the trustee has mixed trust funds with his own. The client and the beneficiaries were therefore entitled to trace into the solicitor's bank account. As there were sufficient funds to meet both claims, it was not necessary to decide which claim had priority. (1880) 13 Ch. D. 696

Space Investments Ltd v. Canadian Imperial Bank of Commerce Trust Co. (Bahamas) 1986

A bank trustee which had the express authority to deposit trust funds with itself did so and subsequently went into liquidation.

HELD: (PC) As the mixing of trust funds with the trustee's own moneys had in this case been entirely lawful and proper, the beneficiaries retained no proprietary interest in the moneys which were deposited with the bank trustee. Accordingly, tracing was not available against the assets of the Bank. [1986] 1 W.L.R. 1072

COMMENTARY

[1] In *Re Hallett's Estate*, Jessel M.R. decided that the solicitor must be presumed to have used his own money before using trust moneys. Thus, the money left in the account must be trust moneys to which the client and the beneficiaries of the settlement were entitled.

[2] The decision of the Privy Council in *Space Investments Ltd. v. Canadian Imperial Bank of Commerce Trust Co. (Bahamas)* should be restricted to situation where the bank is also a trustee. This restriction was suggested by Lord Mustill in *Re Goldcorp Exchange* (above). It is also necessary for the bank trustee to have received express authorisation to deposit the trust moneys with itself .

KEY PRINCIPLE: *The rule in Re Hallett's Estate is subject to the principle that until all the trust moneys are restored, the beneficiary has a first charge over all the assets purchased with money from the bank account.*

Re Oatway 1903

The testator and M were co-trustees under a will. Trust monies were later paid into the testator's own bank account which contained some of his own money. He used some money from the account to purchase shares and subsequently dissipated the rest of the moneys in the account. The testator died insolvent and the shares were subsequently sold. The question arose as to whether the beneficiaries were entitled to trace into the proceeds of sale of the shares.

HELD: (Ch.) The trust had a first charge over the proceeds of sale of the shares. The beneficiaries' claim had to be satisfied before that of the creditors. [1903] 2 Ch. 356.

COMMENTARY

Joyce J. stated (at 360) that " . . . when any money drawn out has been invested, and the investment remains in the name or under the control of the trustee, the rest of the balance having been dissipated by him, he cannot maintain that the investment which remains represent his own money alone, and that what has been spent and can no longer be traced and recovered was money belonging to the trust". Joyce J. went on to say that in these circumstances, the order of priority of payments and withdrawals from the account is immaterial. This represents an exception to *Re Hallett's Estate*, above.

KEY PRINCIPLE: *Where the trustee has mixed trust moneys with his own moneys and subsequently draws out more than his own money therefore spending some of the trust moneys, any subsequent moneys paid in will not be subject to tracing.*

James Roscoe (Bolton) Ltd v. Winder 1915

W purchased the business of a company and one of the terms of the agreement was that W would collect some of the debts of the business and pay them over to the company. The debts amounting to £623 were collected by W. He paid £455 of this into his bank account. He then withdrew all the moneys standing to his credit from the account but left £25 in the account. The money was used it for his own purposes. Later, he paid some money into the account and when he died, there was a credit balance of £358 in the account. The company claimed a charge over this money.

HELD: (Ch) The company was only entitled to a charge over the £25 which had not been withdrawn. [1915] 1 Ch. 62

COMMENTARY

It was decided that where a trustee or fiduciary pays money into his own bank account and withdraws money from it but subsequently pays in more money, it cannot be presumed that the money which was paid in later was intended to replace the trust moneys. Where the trust moneys have been spent, tracing is only available against the trust moneys which remained ("the lower intermediate balance" rule).

KEY PRINCIPLE: *Where trust money has been mixed with the trustee's or the volunteer's own moneys, the beneficiary can claim any profit arising from the investment to the extent*

*to which the trust moneys were used in the acquisition of the
investment.*

Re Tilley's Will Trusts 1967

A testator appointed his wife as one of the executors, giving her
a life interest in his estate with remainder to his son and
daughter in equal shares. After his death in 1932, his widow
redeemed the mortgage on some of the testator's property
using £513 of her own money. By 1952, £2,237 was accumulated as trust capital and over this period of time had mixed her
own money with moneys belonging to the trust. In 1945, she
had an overdraft of £23,536. The daughter died in 1955 and
the plaintiff was her personal representative. The widow died
in 1959. The plaintiff applied for an order that the daughter's
estate should by virtue of her half interest in the testator's estate
have half the proportion of the profits of the purchases made by
the widow to the extent to which the defendants who were the
widow's personal representatives could not establish that these
were bought with her own money. The defendants claimed that
the plaintiff was only entitled to a charge on the widow's bank
account for half the trust moneys plus interest.

HELD: (Ch.) As the trust moneys were not used to purchase
assets but to reduce her overdraft at the bank, tracing could not
be used. [1967] Ch. 1179

COMMENTARY
Ungoed Thomas J. suggested *obiter*, that where there are
profits arising from the use of trust moneys in breach of trust,
the beneficiary could adopt the investment and retain the
profits arising from it to the extent to which the investment
had been acquired through the use of trust moneys.

KEY PRINCIPLE: *Where trust moneys had been used to pay
the premiums of an insurance policy, the beneficiaries can
only recover the premiums plus interest if the beneficial interest in the policy has been assigned to third parties.*

Foskett v. Mckeown 1997

M misappropriated money entrusted to him for purchasing
land in Portugal. Part of this money was used by M to pay
some of the premiums of his life insurance policy. Prior to the
payment being made he had divested the beneficial interest in

the policy to his three children. M later committed suicide. The plaintiff, who was one of the prospective purchasers, claimed to be entitled to the proceeds of the policy. It was decided at first instance, that the purchasers were entitled to 53.46 per cent of the proceeds of the policy.

HELD: (CA) As M did not possess any beneficial interest in the insurance policy at the time the misappropriated money was used to pay the premiums, the proceeds of the policy were not impressed with a resulting or constructive trust. The purchasers were only entitled to recover the money used to pay for the premiums plus interest. [1997] 3 All E.R. 392

COMMENTARY
The Court of Appeal was of the view that the authorities were against the conclusion that the payment of the premiums meant that the payer became the owner of the policy.

INDEX